POLITICAL REALITIES
Edited on behalf of the Politics Association by
Bernard Crick and Derek Heater

Law, Justice and Politics

Second edition

Gavin Drewry
Lecturer in Government,
Bedford College, University of London

Longman

LONGMAN GROUP LIMITED
Longman House
Burnt Mill, Harlow, Essex, UK

First published 1975
Second edition 1981
ISBN 0 582 35329 7

Set in 10/12 pt Times
by Syarikat Seng Teik Sdn. Bhd., Kuala Lumpur, Malaysia.

Printed in Hong Kong by
Commonwealth Printing Press Ltd

Contents

Acknowledgements   iv

Figures and Tables   v

Political Realities: the nature of the series   vi

Preface   viii

Preface to the second edition   ix

1   Law and Politics   1

2   Law, Justice and Morality   14

3   Varieties and Sources of English Law   23

4   Courts and Lawyers   46

5   Administrative Law   73

6   The Law and Freedom of Expression   91

7   Prosecution and Defence   107

8   Justice – and Obstacles to Getting It   123

9   The Cost of the Law   139

Appendix 1: Looking up Legal Sources   158

Appendix 2: The Royal Commission on Legal Services   161

Appendix 3: The Royal Commission on Criminal Procedure   164

Notes and References   165

Bibliography   173

Index   177

Acknowledgements

We are grateful to the following for permission to reproduce copyright material:
Fabian Society for two extracts from their *Research Pamphlet* No. 273; Guardian Newspapers Ltd for an extract from the article "What's wrong with the law: rush to judgement" from *The Guardian* 7th October 1971 and an extract from a report of a speech by Norman Atkinson M.P. from *The Guardian* 18th April 1972; The Controller of Her Majesty's Stationery Office for the Map "Circuits, High Court and Crown Centres for England and Wales" from *Britain* 1973; The New Law Journal for an extract from the Editor's conversation with the Lord Chancellor from *New Law Journal* 1st January 1970 and two extracts from the article "Do we need a Ministry of Justice?" by A. Samuels from *New Law Journal* 11th February 1971; New Science Publications for an extract from the article "The Tribunals of the Welfare State" by P. Harrison from *New Society* London 22nd November 1973, The Weekly Review of the Social Sciences; Penguin Books Ltd for extracts from *Freedom, the Individual and the Law* 3rd edition by H. Street; Sweet and Maxwell Ltd for the table headed "Sentences imposed in Magistrates' Courts and numbers and percentages of Defendants represented" from the article "The Undefended Defendant in Criminal Courts" by Michael Zander which appeared in *Criminal Law Review* 1969 and the *Sunday Times* for an extract from an article by Lord Devlin from *Sunday Times* 2nd July 1972 and an extract from a feature by Lord Goodman from *Sunday Times* 12th June 1966.

Figures and Tables

Fig. 3.1   Principal categories of law

Fig. 4.1   Outline of the English court structure

Fig. 4.2   Circuits: High Court and crown court centres for England and Wales

Table 4.1   The six circuits: summary

Table 4.2   The judiciary

Table 9.1   Calculating Civil Legal Aid – Eligibility and Contributions

Table 9.2   Sentences imposed in magistrates' courts and numbers and percentages of defendants represented

Political Realities:
the nature of the series

A great need is felt for short books which can supplement or even replace textbooks and which can deal in an objective but realistic way with problems that arouse political controversy. The series aims to break from a purely descriptive and institutional approach to one that will show how and why there are different interpretations both of how things work and how they ought to work. Too often in the past "British Constitution" has been taught quite apart from any knowledge of the actual political conflicts which institutions strive to contain. So the Politics Association sponsors this new series because it believes that a specifically civic education is an essential part of any liberal or general education, but that respect for political rules and an active citizenship can only be encouraged by helping pupils, students and young voters to discover what are the main objects of political controversy, the varying views about the nature of the constitution – themselves often highly political – and what are the most widely canvassed alternative policies in their society. From such a realistic appreciation of differences and conflicts reasoning can then follow about the common processes of containing or resolving them peacefully.

The specific topics chosen are based on an analysis of the main elements in existing "A" level syllabuses, and the manner in which they are treated is based on the conviction of the editors that almost every examination board is moving, slowly but surely, away from a concentration on constitutional rules and towards a more difficult but important concept of a realistic political education or the enhancement of political literacy.

This approach has, of course, been common enough in the universities for many years. Quite apart from its civic importance, the teaching of politics in schools has tended to lag behind university practice and expectations. So the editors have aimed to draw on the most up-to-date academic knowledge, with some of the books being written by university teachers, some by secondary or further education teachers, but both aware of the skills and knowledge of the other.

The Politics Association and the editors are conscious of the great importance of other levels of education, and are actively pursuing studies and projects of curriculum development in several directions, particularly towards CSE needs; but it was decided to begin with "A" level and new developments in sixth-form courses precisely because of the great overlap here between teaching in secondary school and further education colleges, whether specifically for examinations or not; indeed most of the books will be equally useful for general studies.

Bernard Crick
Derek Heater

Preface

This is a book, about aspects of law, intended primarily for politics students, though with the interests of those studying English law also borne in mind. It is not intended to be a legal reference book, though it has been necessary to include some descriptive matter for the sake of coherence.

Given the limited scope many interesting and potentially relevant things have had to be left out. There has been no room, for example, to discuss penal policy and sentencing; the politico-legal aspects of public order have only been touched upon. The author can only express his regret and refer the reader to the short bibliography and to the bibliographies in the works cited there.

One word of warning is necessary in using a work of this kind. The rights and wrongs of the arguments about legal reform are far from clearcut. Here they have been greatly simplified; some critics may feel that I have been too inconoclastic, others that I have been mealy-mouthed. I have cited research evidence where possible, but it should be pointed out that a great deal of work remains to be done. Not everyone, for example, unreservedly accepts the validity of the research carried out by the indefatigable Michael Zander, but most of his critics have yet to produce evidence (other than of a very impressionistic kind) to refute him.

I should like to thank all those who assisted in the preparation of this book, subject to the usual disclaimer that they are in no way to blame for its shortcomings. Mr Keith Eddey of Oxford Polytechnic generously gave time to rescue me from many pitfalls confronting a non-lawyer writing about law. Colleagues at Bedford College, Dr Ivor Burton, Louis Blom-Cooper, QC, and Mrs Jenny Brock, helpfully suggested improvements to the final draft, as did Professor Bernard Crick of Birkbeck College. Finally, my thanks to Miss Sally Adams who both typed and tidied the manuscript.

Gavin Drewry, Bedford College, May 1974

Preface to the second edition

The first edition of this book was written in 1974. A great deal has happened since then and a substantial revision has become necessary. I say "substantial" rather than "fundamental" because the subject-matter and its arrangement remains largely unchanged (and law, by its very nature, does not alter fundamentally in six years – or in sixty.)

Apart from updating facts and figures to do with judicial salaries, financial limits for legal aid, maximum penalties, etc., many parts of the text have had to be completely rewritten to take account of developments in such matters as local law centres, police complaints machinery, bail, recent judicial decisions in the field of administrative law, and pronouncements by the European Court of Justice. Continuing debate about such things as jury-vetting, telephone tapping, open government, and the need for a UK Bill of Rights has also been taken into account in this revision, though inevitably lack of space has meant that none of them has been given the fullness of treatment that it deserves. In some places, to avoid expensive re-setting, I have merely indicated a recent development or an up-to-date source of reference in an appropriate footnote. Two highly relevant Royal Commissions are dealt with as separate appendices; eventually, if and when their reports have been debated and implemented (or not), they will have to be assimilated into the text of a third edition of this book.

In undertaking this revision I have benefited greatly from the constructive comments of reviewers and teaching colleagues. Though intended mainly for students in sixth forms and Colleges of Further Education I have been gratified to find that the book has also been used fairly widely at degree level and by law students; with this in mind I have taken the opportunity to update and expand the bibliography.

Gavin Drewry
Bedford College, April 1980

Note: The information in this book takes account of events up to the end of April 1980, but some alterations have been made in the light of important occurrences in the summer and autumn of 1980. In November 1980, as this edition was about to go to press, the Government announced the renewal of the right of individual UK citizens to petition the European Commission on Human Rights, for a period of five years from January 1981. The legislative programme of the 1980–81 parliamentary session included government Bills to abolish the notorious ''sus'' law and to make extensive changes to the law on contempt of court.

1 Law and Politics

Where laws end, tyrannies begin.

WILLIAM PITT on the Wilkes case

When the state is most corrupt, then laws are most multiplied.

TACITUS

Readers of this book may be forgiven for wondering what the study of politics has to do with law. Modern textbooks on British government tend to do no more than make very cursory reference to the structure of the courts and to the part played by judges in curbing administrative transgressions.

The answer is that law is an essential part of politics. When we stop to think what government is all about we very quickly come up against words like "power", "authority" and (in Bernard Crick's phrase) "adjustment to diversity".[1] The legal system supplies an orderly means for the settlement of disputes in the state; the criminal law sets minimum standards of conduct and provides legitimate machinery for dealing with those who offend against the wellbeing of their fellow citizens and against the state itself. The law is the means by which the violence which underpins the *power* of the state is sublimated into recognition of the legitimacy of the state's *authority*.

The existence of law is what distinguishes a stable, viable state from a situation of anarchy. The great seventeenth-century political philosopher, Thomas Hobbes, depicted the state as founded upon a social contract (itself a legal concept) in which men agree to accept the rule of an absolute sovereign rather than live in a "state of nature" where liberty means lawlessness and an ever-present fear of a knife in the back:

The final cause, end, or design of men, who naturally love liberty, and dominion over others, in the introduction of that restraint upon themselves, in which we see them live in commonwealths, is the foresight of their own preservation, and of a more contented life thereby; that is to say, of getting themselves out from that miserable condition of war, which is necessarily consequent . . . to the natural passions of men, when there is no visible power to keep them in awe, and tie them by fear of punishment to the performance of their covenants.[2]

At a more practical level, when political decisions come to be translated into legal rules, things do not come to a full stop when an Act of Parliament receives its royal assent; a policy can stand or fall by the approach adopted towards a new Act by the judges called upon to interpret and apply it. Every year the government brings in a Finance Bill, embodying its main economic and fiscal policies. When the Act is passed, there are myriads of taxpayers waiting in the wings, eager to reduce their own tax liability. Tax law is not just a matter of the government getting its Bill through Parliament, it is a constant running battle between the Inland Revenue on the one hand and the taxpayer on the other, with the courts continually arbitrating between the two sides and Parliament having to plug the holes in legislation exposed by the pronouncements of the judges.

Moreover, a great deal of political activity, particularly at a grass-roots level, serves to obscure still further the distinction between law and politics. Many community rights and civil rights pressure groups, for example, are anxious both to ensure that people receive their rights under existing law and to do everything they can to see that defects in that law are remedied. Thus advice is commonly given to tenants about their legal rights, while the people giving the advice are also waging a political war against the unfair practices of local landlords and the infirmity of existing legislation in the field of housing.

In December 1973 it was reported that Kensington and Chelsea Council had threatened to withdraw its financial support from the North Kensington Neighbourhood Law Centre because of the latter's involvement in local political campaigns. In matters like landlord and tenant law and "poverty law", involving chronically underprivileged sections of the community, many lawyers acknowledge that it is impossible to draw a hard and fast distinction between a legalistic concern with what the law is and the political question of what it ought to be.

To sum up: it is wholly misleading to see the political process as something wholly separate from the legal process, there is constant interaction between the two. And "government" is a composite activity which embraces both.

Separation of powers

The supposed separateness of law and politics has been underlined by references in many books on constitutional law to the "separation of powers" which is said to characterise the institutional arrangements of British government. Such separation is alleged to be a good thing in so far as it prevents the overconcentration of power in any one institution. The proposition that British government is founded on a formal separation of the "legislative", "executive" and "judicial" aspects of government goes back to the writings of the French philosopher Montesquieu, and in particular to his *De l'esprit des Lois*, first published in 1748.

There is now a fairly general consensus that Montesquieu was guilty of oversimplification and that governmental functions cannot be compartmentalised in this way. Even in countries like the United States, with written constitutions containing provisions for separation of powers, things do not work out quite so neatly.

There is a substantial body of literature on the subject, much of it confused and contradictory. As Geoffrey Marshall says:

The phrase "separation of powers" is . . . one of the most confusing in the vocabulary of political and constitutional thought. . . . It crops up . . . in discussions, for example, of judicial independence, delegation of legislative powers, executive responsibility to legislatures, judicial review [of administrative actions], and constitutionality of arbitral bodies exercising mixed functions [e.g. administrative tribunals and inquiries]. It is possible, indeed commonplace, for commentators to draw different conclusions both as to whether there is or is not a separation of powers in a given constitution and as to what particular conclusions of law or policy follow from the existence of a separation of powers, even where it is admitted to exist.[3]

It is not possible to undertake a detailed review of the arguments here. It has already been emphasised that the process of making legislation is interwoven with the judicial function of interpreting and applying that legislation. A living refutation of the doctrine of separation of powers can be found in the office of the Lord Chancellor: he is a Cabinet minister, he presides over the sittings of the House of Lords in its legislative and deliberative capacities, he can sit as a judge, he appoints other judges and he runs a government department.

The point is that there are some aspects of "separation of powers" which are eminently sensible. For example, it is probably a good idea to have a judiciary which is somewhat aloof from the rough and tumble of party politics. And words like "legislative", "executive" and "judicial" are a useful shorthand way of describing a lot of things that go on in government, provided we remember that the boundaries between them are indistinct and that they are all functionally interrelated.

Above all, it is important to avoid being mesmerised into believing that "separation of powers" has some mystical virtue as an iron law of the constitution and as a yardstick against which the merits of institutional arrangements can be measured. We have no written constitution, and British government is not based on immutable laws. Thus it is wholly misguided to suggest, as students sometimes do, that the growth of delegated legislation or the proliferation of administrative tribunals is to be deplored as being in breach of the "doctrine of separation of powers".

Legalism

Belief in a doctrine of separation of powers merely symptomises a common view that law and politics are two quite different things. Judith Shklar, a professor of politics at Harvard, stresses the existence of an ideology that she calls "legalism". This consists of a belief in the merits of rule-following and the pursuit of certainty which characterises the legal process. She continues:

There appears to be a virtually unanimous agreement that law and politics must be kept apart as much as possible in theory no less than in practice. The divorce of law from politics is, to be sure, designed to prevent arbitrariness, and that is why there is so little argument about its necessity. However, ideologically legalism does not stop there. Politics is regarded not only as something apart from law but as inferior to law. Law aims at justice, while politics looks only to expediency. The former is neutral and objective, the latter is the uncontrolled child of competing interests and ideologies.[4]

The supposed superiority of "good clean law" over "bad dirty politics" manifests itself in all kinds of ways. There is, for example, a rather ill-defined area of law-cum-politics called administrative law (see chapter 5), which is concerned with defining and applying a framework of legal rules to the activities of administrators and policy-makers. In this context people seem sometimes to make the tacit assumption that making administrators subject to law will, by the very nature of law as something "above politics" (that is, above partisanship and intrigue), make the world a better place. In practice, as we shall see, the converse may be the case; the essential flexibility of the administrative process may well be damaged by the superimposition of lawyers' precedents and obsessions with due process at the expense of substantive justice.

Often when governments get into some kind of trouble or when there is a great national calamity, politicians set up a tribunal of inquiry presided over by a senior judge. The philosophy that lies behind this course of action is (*a*) that judges are professionally experienced in getting at the truth, and (*b*) that they are above suspicions of partisanship. The former proposition has some truth, though it is questionable whether the sort of experience that judges have is particularly relevant to discovering whether civil servants should have intervened earlier to prevent the collapse of a motor insurance company or whether the National Coal Board should have taken steps to prevent the calamitous collapse of a waste tip on a mountainside in Wales.[5]

The second proposition also has a good deal of truth, but is to some extent self-refuting. Once judges are brought into the political arena in this way they become more closely associated in the public mind with "politics", particularly if their findings tend to favour the government's position. The moral would seem to be that judicial inquiries play a useful part in calming public fears, but using them too frequently can only be self-defeating.

Even if "separation of powers" is only a half-truth, it is important to bear in mind that a degree of "separateness" is maintained by those actually involved in the various tasks of government. Thus the courts acknowledge the sovereignty of Parliament by accepting as binding every piece of legislation that is passed (though, as we shall see, there are devices by which judges can sometimes avoid aspects of legislation with which they disagree); in doing so they look only at the legislation itself and not at any supporting evidence of Parliament's intentions, such as the *Hansard* reports of debates on the original Bill.

In its turn, Parliament is bound by a self-imposed *sub judice* rule, which means that, with some exceptions, it cannot debate anything going on in the courts until legal proceedings are completed. There is considerable value in such a rule, but it tends in practice to operate too inflexibly.[6]

The rule of law

There is, as we have seen, a tendency to treat "separation of powers" as a doctrine which underpins good government; the same can be said of the phrase "rule of law". The latter is associated principally with the writings of the great constitutional lawyer A.V. Dicey, whose works were much in vogue at the beginning of this century and are still worth reading today. Dicey's concern was with equality before the law, with "the idea of legality or of the universal subjection of all classes to one law administered by the ordinary courts".[7] In particular, he wanted no distinction in law between the citizen and servants of the state, and viewed with dismay the prospect that English law might become contaminated by the systems of "administrative law" prevalent on the Continent, which seemed to him to place government officials in a privileged legal position.

In fact Dicey misunderstood the significance of these continental institutions. Certainly there are systems of administrative law (*droit administratif*) in countries like France, but, far from giving officials favoured treatment, they provide additional legal curbs on the government, over and above the ordinary law, and give the private citizen special legal rights and remedies vis-à-vis officialdom.

Dicey's exaggerated fears about administrative law (though he modified his views in later writings) account for some of the early hostility expressed by lawyers to such innovations as administrative tribunals (see chapter 5). Moreover, his ideas about the "rule of law" have acquired a mystical quality which they hardly merit. It is one thing to use an expression like this to abbreviate some complex ideas about law and government, but it is misleading to treat it as having some absolute value. Rule of law has become part of the rhetoric of political debate; it is quite common to hear politicians proclaiming a "threat to the rule of law" when all they mean is that a political demonstration has got out of hand.

There is much to be commended in a political system which stresses the importance of an independent judiciary and such values as equality before the law, though, as we shall see later, some categories of people are more equal than others. But there is also a very strong case for saying that the last thing we want is to be *ruled* by law; law is there to provide a framework of order and justice but it is a *product* of the political process, not the other way round.

Northern Ireland

As we have seen, law is the medium through which the state exercises its authority. What happens when the consensus and stability that characterises the state begin to crumble at the edges? What happens when a substantial section of the population denies the legitimacy of the established order and when rule formerly based on recognition of authority gives way to rule through the mobilisation of the naked power of the state? These questions are of crucial relevance in the context of the present troubles in Northern Ireland.

We have noted that, even in conditions of peace and stability, it is impossible to make a firm distinction between law and politics; this is true *a fortiori* in a situation verging on civil war. The IRA has refused to recognise the legitimacy either of the Protestant-dominated Northern Ireland Parliament or of the system of direct rule from Westminster which superseded it in March 1972.

There is a tendency in official quarters to treat the trial of terrorists in Northern Ireland (and in England for that matter)[8] as a simple extension of the criminal trial process. One can well understand the authorities being reluctant to endow offences of terrorism with an aura of romantic military adventure; many such offences are, by any rational standards, sordid acts of brutal criminality. However, some allowance must surely be made for the fact that many of the people being tried for these offences sincerely regard themselves as engaged in rightful (not lawful) combat. In other words, there comes a point where the state must acknowledge that it has a war on its hands (though there are understandable reasons why such an admission tends to be postponed for as long as is possible) and that the *political* issues underlying the conflict cannot simply be reduced to the dichotomy of "right" versus "wrong" which is implicit in the ordinary process of criminal trial.

Some modifications have indeed been made to the machinery of justice in Northern Ireland. Suspected terrorists can, subject to certain safeguards, be detained in custody after a hearing before legally qualified Commissioners which bears little resemblance to a criminal trial. This system of detention superseded the even more summary process of internment instituted by the Stormont Government. The Northern Ireland (Emergency Provisions) Act 1973 provided, among other things, for serious crimes to be tried without a jury and for the normal rules of evidence to be relaxed in such cases.

So some acknowledgment has been made of the special circumstances of Northern Ireland but the basic difference of perception between the terrorists and the authorities has not been institutionalised. The government sees the new arrangements as a means of curbing escalating terrorist crimes; the extremists still believe that they are fighting a political war which the authorities cannot or will not understand.

Lawyers and politics
In his book, *The New Anatomy of Britain*, Anthony Sampson writes:

> Lawyers have excelled in politics, but not often reached the peak. The last career barrister to become prime minister was Asquith: the last (and only) solicitor was Lloyd George. The only law officer who ever became prime minister was Spencer Percival in 1809, and he was shot dead two years later. But nevertheless lawyers – more than any other profession – have gravitated to politics, and barristers now [in 1971] make up almost a sixth of the House of Commons: 93 of them, compared to only 78 in 1966. For successful barristers politics has been a natural climax, and they have been able to combine a lucrative practice with a prominent political career. It is most doubtful nowadays whether this close connection can continue. Both careers are more specialised

and professional: to maintain a successful bar practice while sitting on the backbenches is much more difficult, and first class barristers are more inclined to keep out of parliament.[9]

Given that, as we have seen, the functions of government cut across the rigid "separation of powers" categories of institutions like the Cabinet, Parliament and the courts, the interchange of personnel between law and politics may serve a useful purpose in facilitating the flow of information between different parts of the governmental machine. If Parliament passes laws which have later to be interpreted and applied by lawyers it is handy to have some of the latter available to give advice.

To the ranks of barristers and solicitors in Parliament must be added the dozen or so Law Lords – the judges who constitute the House of Lords when it sits judicially – who play an important part in expressing the judicial viewpoint in Parliament on a wide range of topics. Having judges in Parliament reduces the tendency for a communications gap to develop between the legislature and the courts.

Concern is expressed from time to time about the risk of judges being too closely associated with party politics (we have already noted the dangers involved in governments being too ready to use judicial inquiries to defuse potential crises). The political and other affiliations of judges have been scrutinised anxiously by academics and others to establish whether they are really qualified to pass themselves off as "neutral" arbiters in matters which have party-political implications or where the scales of justice are being held between the state on the one hand and a private citizen, or a group of citizens, on the other.

The question is sometimes asked whether the appointment of judges is free from party bias. Of course, even if we could demonstrate such bias it would remain for us to prove that it tainted the decisions that judges reach; but, given the essentially subjective quality of substantive justice, it is probably fair to say that evidence of potential bias would do much to erode the citizen's confidence in the fairness of the courts.

Up to the 1920s it was the accepted practice for Lord Chancellors to treat judgeships, or at least some of them, as rewards for political services. Harold Laski, writing in the 1930s, showed that of 139 appointments to the higher judiciary between 1832 and 1906, eighty judges were MPs at the time of their appointment, and sixty-three of those eighty were appointed when their own party was in power.[10] Lord Halsbury, Conservative Lord Chancellor 1886–92 and again 1895–1905, acquired particular notoriety for the partisan nature of his appointments, though the case against him has been weakened by recent researches.[11]

But certainly there was once a fairly general belief that the political affiliations of judges should be a relevant factor in judicial appointments and promotions. This was particularly evident at the turn of the century at a time when the activities of the state were expanding at an unprecedented rate, confronting the courts with new and unfamiliar problems, though, as we shall see in chapter 7, many problems later to be associated with the welfare state and the managed economy were, from the start, taken out of the hands of the courts and entrusted to specialised tribunals. This was also a politically sensitive period in so far as the Labour Party and the trade unions were coming into their own as a potent political force in competition with the established parties.

. In 1911 Robson, the Attorney-General, wrote to Asquith, the Liberal Prime Minister, asking for the appointment of more Law Lords from the ranks of the Liberal Party. He pointed out that the House of Lords in its judicial capacity,

> would have to play a great part in disputes that are legal in form but political in fact, and it would be idle to deny the resolute bias of the Judges – there and elsewhere. That bias will probably operate more than ever in cases that touch on labour, educational, constitutional and, for the future I might perhaps add, revenue questions.[12]

In a system where it is recognised that senior judgeships are perks of political loyalty the Robson solution – make sure that there is an even party balance on the Bench – is probably the most appropriate. The alternative is to get rid of the party-political factor altogether. According to Professors Abel-Smith and Stevens:

> Sankey, who became Lord Chancellor in 1929, was determined not to follow the tradition of appointing persons with political experience as law lords . . . the opportunity was used in the period

between 1928 and 1932 to replace politically appointed law lords with the now more traditional professional type of judge.[13]

This new policy, say the authors, coincided with a more restrained judicial approach to questions of public law.

Despite the virtual disappearance of crudely partisan judicial appointments there has been frequent speculation about the political bias of the judges, particularly towards trade unions. Harold Laski was one of the most vigorous Labour critics of the "spoils" system; in 1946 Aneurin Bevan made it clear that the Labour Government would allow no "judicial sabotage of its legislation". More recently, the operation of the Industrial Relations Court had revived the suspicions of the Labour Movement about the inbuilt bias of the judiciary. In May 1977 there was fresh controversy when Michael Foot complained that trade unions had always had a raw deal from the courts.

The fact is that judges *cannot* be "neutral"; every human being is biased. Fears about political patronage in higher judicial appointments no longer causes much concern and may indeed have missed the point anyway. What is more worrying is the inbuilt conservatism of the legal profession, a product both of social background and of professional training. This conservatism undermines the *appearance* of neutrality in the judicial process; it is a point we shall return to in chapter 8. It is clear, moreover, that judges are ("separation of powers" notwithstanding) close to the governing "Establishment"

Moreover, there is still a relic of political patronage at the bottom end of the judicial hierarchy, in magistrates' courts. Magistrates, considered individually, do not make decisions of major social or legal importance, but collectively, by sheer weight of numbers, they have a substantial influence on the lives of millions of people. The methods of appointing magistrates have always been a matter of serious concern.

The case for a ministry of justice
The case for setting up a ministry of justice was set out in the Haldane Report on the Machinery of Government in 1918,[14] and has been the subject of sporadic debate ever since. The Haldane Committee pointed out the weaknesses of a system where responsibility for the legal functions of government are split between the Lord Chancellor (who appointed judges, and administered the civil courts and some

criminal courts), the Home Secretary (responsible for some aspects of criminal law, the police and the penal system), and the Law Officers' departments (sharing with the Lord Chancellor the task of giving legal advice to the government, and representing the government in legal proceedings). The greatest gap was then, and still is, the lack of a ministry with clearcut responsibility for law reform.

The Haldane proposals for fashioning a ministry of justice out of the legal-administrative functions of the Lord Chancellor and the Home Secretary were warmly welcomed by the Law Society (the statutory body administering the solicitors' branch of the legal profession) but condemned out of hand by the Bar Council, which feared that judicial appointments might be made on a partisan basis by a political minister in the Commons. (In fact Haldane's proposal would have left judicial appointments in the hands of the Lord Chancellor, though others, including the minister of justice, would have been called upon to advise him.)

There was, moreover, a widespread view that, while ministries of justice thrive on the Continent, where judges traditionally work within a bureaucratic career structure, the system might interfere with our tradition of appointing judges from among practising barristers and letting them learn the judicial arts on the job.

The Haldane proposal has never been implemented, even though Haldane himself had another brief spell as Lord Chancellor in 1924 and could presumably have pushed it through had he been willing and able to do so. From 1964 to 1966 Sir Eric Fletcher was Minister without Portfolio, with special responsibility for law reform and justice, but this experiment was abandoned without explanation.

Lord Scarman, when he was chairman of the Law Commission, remarked on the grave disadvantage of not having a minister to steer law reform proposals through the Commons. Many commentators have alluded to the ludicrous overburdening of the office of Lord Chancellor who, in theory, is expected to be in umpteen very different places simultaneously and to be non-partisan in some contexts while remaining a government minister. This role conflict was heavily underlined by criticisms of some allegedly very partisan remarks by Lord Hailsham in defence of the President of the Industrial Relations Court in December 1973.

The case was cogently put by Alec Samuels in an article, "Do we need a Ministry of Justice?", in the *New Law Journal*, 11 February

1971. On the one hand he applauded the potential "dynamism of a minister who would be responsible for law reform"; on the other, he suggested that the Lord Chancellor's Department was already doing the job of a ministry of justice and that a new ministry would mean new demarcation problems. He suggested that "the practice of renaming, merging and creating ministries has done little if anything to improve the social and economic life of the country. There is little or nothing to be gained from shuffling around the same people." There is truth in this, but surely it depends upon the form that the new ministry would take? It is rather defeatist to assume that it would have to be a revamped version of what we have already got.

The creation of the Law Commission in 1965 has undoubtedly given a clearer focus to the task of law reform; and the Courts Act 1971 has markedly rationalised the machinery for administering the courts, giving the Lord Chancellor's Department more, and more clearly defined, responsibilities in the field. In March 1980 it assumed responsibilities for criminal legal aid formerly exercised by the Home Office. The problem of judicial appointments remains; diminished by the end of party patronage, but enhanced by the ever increasing number of judges (and chairmen of tribunals, etc) that have to be appointed. This problem would not be solved by the kind of ministry envisaged by Haldane. Nevertheless, Lord Scarman's remarks about the inadequacies of the machinery for implementing law reform cannot lightly be brushed aside.

2 Law, Justice and Morality

A long line of cases has shown that it is not merely a matter of some importance, but it is of fundamental importance, that justice should not only be done, but should manifestly and undoubtedly be seen to be done.

LORD CHIEF JUSTICE HEWART

What is law?

Let it be said straight away that if anyone were to state categorically that he knew the precise answer to the question "what is law?" he would deserve to be regarded either as a fool or as the greatest philosopher living. The universal problem about defining terms is that the process of definition is essentially arbitrary. If I use the word "law" in conversation I naturally expect it to convey a meaning to the person to whom I am talking; but unless I am careful and, above all, *consistent* in the way I use a word of this kind I may find myself at cross-purpose with someone who has a totally different conception of what law really is.

The word law is used in contexts which have nothing to do with the subject matter of this book. One frequently encounters expressions like "the laws of nature", "the law of gravity" and "the laws of cricket". If this were a treatise on linguistic philosophy it would be possible to trace all kinds of fascinating links between these usages of the word "law" and the kind of law that is found in the solicitor's office or the courtroom. But, for our present purposes, I shall echo the arrogant retort of Humpty Dumpty in *Alice Through the Looking Glass* that a word "means what I choose it to mean – neither more nor less". As good a working definition as any is that to be found in the *Shorter Oxford English Dictionary* under the subheading "Human law": "the body of rules, whether formally enacted or customary, which a state or community recognises as binding on its members or subjects".

Having airily waved aside a definitional problem which has been baffling legal philosophers for centuries, let us now turn to the even more difficult problem of reconciling "law" with "justice".

Law and justice

In 1939 the rector of a rural parish rented a small piece of land from his neighbours for a nominal rent of ten shillings a year. After 1942 the neighbours ceased to ask for any rent and the rector, and his successors, continued to use the land as part of their garden. In 1960 the then rector started to negotiate the sale of his land – and added to it the neighbours' portion of the garden. The neighbours, who had been devout members of the church and would not have dreamed of asking even for a nominal rent from the rector, brought an action for possession of the land, which they said had always been theirs.

They won their case in the county court, but the rector appealed to the Court of Appeal. He relied on what is called the rule of "adverse possession", arguing that since he and his predecessors had used the land for so long without being asked for rent the original owners' title to it had expired. Examining the relevant authorities the Court had reluctantly to agree that he had a good case in law; but the judges made it clear in no uncertain terms what they thought about the merits of the rector's action. Here is an extract from the judgment of Lord Justice Davies:

The plaintiffs [i.e. the neighbours] had an indisputable paper title to this piece of land. The plaintiffs . . . had . . . forborne to demand the rent of 10s a year; and the reason for their forbearance was their loyalty and generosity to their church. As [the plaintiff] said in evidence, if the rector had given him ten shillings he would have put it in the offertory box. . . .

An appeal was brought to this court. At the end of the hearing the court indicated its strong views on the merits of the case and reserved its judgment in order that the matter should be further considered by the Church authorities, in the hope that wiser, more generous and more Christian counsels should prevail. . . .

But . . . the rector . . . wanted his "pound of flesh". In the absence of a Portia to help us, he must in my judgment have it.[1]

The moral of this case is that "law" and "justice" are often two quite different things. When Shylock demanded his pound of flesh, Portia warned him:

"For, as thou urgest justice, be assured
Thou shalt have justice, more than thou desir'st."

Both Shylock and the rector's neighbours must have come away from the courts with a very jaundiced view of what "justice" had to offer them.

The difficulty arises mainly from the confusion of two quite distinct senses in which the word justice is used. The first sense is what might be termed *procedural* justice, which has to do with the following of the rules laid down for the proper conduct of legal business (what the Fifth and Fourteenth Amendments to the United States Constitution call "due process of law"). The second is *substantive* justice which has to do with the observer's subjective impression of the fairness of the outcome. Many lawyers use the word justice to mean that someone has had a fair trial and that (adopting Lord Hewart's phrase quoted at the beginning of this chapter) he and everyone else can *see* that he has had a fair trial. But knowing that one has had a fair trial is hardly much comfort to someone whose land is taken from him by a quirk of the law.

Legal philosophy in medieval times was dominated by a belief in *natural law*, epitomised in the writings of a great thirteenth-century theologian, St Thomas Aquinas. This school of philosophy (which is nowadays rather out of fashion) held that God had ordained a body of laws, knowable by divinely inspired law-makers, to which human laws should conform. To a believer in natural law it may well appear that a law is unjust because it does not accord with God's law. However, many lawyers nowadays are *positivists*; they argue that their business is not with whether a law is right or wrong, just or unjust, but whether it derives from a competent source (that is, from an Act of Parliament or from a binding precedent). Their job, they argue, is to decide what the law *is*, and not what it *ought* to be. Max Weber pointed out the tendency for lawyers in Western societies to emphasise "formal rationality" (due process) at the expense of "substantive rationality" (concern for substantive justice in particular cases).

Judges who pursue substantive justice at the expense of due process tend to be regarded by their fellow lawyers as sentimental nuisances who undermine the essential certainty and consistency of the legal process; this is one of the side-effects of the doctrine of precedent, discussed in chapter 3.

There tends to be a communication gap between lawyers and non-lawyers: the former stress the "fairness" of the legal process while the latter tend to look at each case on its merits to see if its outcome accords with a subjective commonsense view of fair play. The gap between procedural and substantive justice tends to be exacerbated by the culture gap that exists between lawyers, with their essentially middle-class orientation, and non-lawyers, particularly those from the working class. This is a problem to which we shall return in chapter 8.

Law and morality

In 1957 the Wolfenden Committee on Homosexuality and Prostitution recommended that homosexual behaviour between consenting adults in private should cease to be a criminal offence. Justifying this recommendation it said:

> We do not think that it is proper for the law to concern itself with what a man does in private unless it can be shown to be so contrary to the public good that the law ought to intervene in its function as the guardian of that public good.[2]

The debate about the extent to which moral beliefs should be written into the law has been going on for a very long time. There are two main schools of thought. There are those who argue that immorality should always be treated as crime because once we start making exceptions this is the thin edge of the wedge which will ultimately bring about the disintegration of society as we know it. Then there is the contrary view which holds that while there are obvious and proper links between morality and the law, there are aspects of human behaviour which, so long as they do not harm other people, should not be legally prohibited even if they are morally wrong (e.g. adultery – see below).

The former view is expressed in the writings of two distinguished English jurists: Sir James Fitzjames Stephen in the nineteenth-century and Lord Devlin in the twentieth. The second viewpoint appears in the writings of John Stuart Mill and, more recently, of Professor H.L.A. Hart, as well as in the Wolfenden Report.

In the end it is a matter of personal judgment and even of ideology. But those who consider that what is immoral should always be illegal face one overwhelming problem. Morality is essentially a subjective commodity and one which has a habit of changing rapidly in a short space of time (witness the rapid fluctuations in the law controlling obscene publications and in public attitudes to these laws). So how can morality be defined and identified for the purpose of turning it into law?

Lord Devlin[3] answers this point, but his solution is unconvincing. His test of morality is to ask the "man on the Clapham omnibus", the average English juryman, what *he* thinks is moral or immoral. This touching faith in the wisdom of the South London commuter is surely misplaced. How is such a jury going to be interrogated on this matter and how sure can we be that it will have understood the question? Is such a jury representative of public opinion (at the time when Lord Devlin wrote this only ratepayers could serve on a jury)? Is there not something rather alarming about a legal system which, if Lord Devlin had his way, could find a man guilty of immorality-cum-crime one week and not guilty the next because of some fickle shift in public opinion? Some would question whether the jury should continue to play any part in the trial process at all, let alone whether its role should be extended from the adjudication of facts to the identification of public morality.

In a case decided in the 1960s, *Shaw* v *D.P.P.*[4], the House of Lords, by a majority, brought out of cold storage a long dormant offence of "conspiracy to corrupt public morals". The case concerned a man who published a directory listing the names and addresses of prostitutes. While the accused person in this case may well have deserved all he got, once we start bending the law to give vent to moral outrage this may be the thin end of the wedge; we may find such a power being used in cases where we are much less certain of the moral position. There is inconsistency on the part of lawyers who claim that the law must be certain and then allow the courts to create special offences to meet special cases.

All kinds of anomalies exist in the relationship between law and morals. Some kinds of behaviour which the law regards as criminal are not seen as such by those who indulge in it. Apart from homosexuals, already mentioned, a large number of motorists come before the courts for offences which they probably regard as carrying none of the stigma of criminality.

It may be argued that a man who gets a parking ticket for parking on a yellow line is, unless he is seriously obstructing others, committing a purely administrative transgression stemming from a policy decision to keep the volume of traffic in towns at an acceptable level. Equally, it may be said that a man who drives his E-type at breakneck speed down a winding country lane is being at least as antisocial as a man who carelessly brandishes a loaded shotgun in a busy street. Yet popular opinion tends to associate shotguns with "real" crime, whereas cars are something that we all know and rely on. Those responsible for enforcing the law, even if they disapprove of reckless driving, can at least personally identify to some extent with the errors of judgment which everyone makes from time to time when they are at the wheel. It may well be that escalating road casualty figures, coupled with a growing antipathy towards motor vehicles as a source of environmental pollution, will harden public attitudes against the reckless and selfish motorist. But it is likely that motoring crime will always be in a class apart in terms of popular morality, if only because so many car owners exist.[5] It is worth contemplating whether, if half the population habitually stole, theft could ever remain a "real" crime.

Just as there are some areas of criminal law which tend to be regarded as set slightly apart from "real" crime so there are some kinds of conduct which are morally condemned but which are not proscribed by the criminal law. The classic instance is adultery which has never been a criminal offence in English common law (though it is treated as a crime in some other countries) even though theologians have always treated it as a sin. In the civil law relating to divorce, however, the law has tended to adopt a punitive attitude towards the adulterer (and, as a good instance of the law's discrimination against women, has been even harsher in its treatment of the adulteress); this is less true since the abolition of the concept of "matrimonial offences" by the Divorce Reform Act 1969, though even under the new law the "guilt" of the parties may sometimes be taken into account in considering ancillary matters like financial maintenance.

To sum up this complicated subject it can only be said that the links between morality and law tend to grow up in an alarmingly haphazard way. There is no consensus about morality and it is inevitable that the moral values that get embodied in the law are those of an atypical elite: lawyers, judges, politicians, and so on. Moreover, the fact that law tends to act as a buffer against rapid social change means that legal rules tend not only to reflect the values of an elite but also to lag behind changes in social outlook. Many of today's laws are thus based on the morality that prevailed in an elite group that held power a generation, or perhaps several generations ago. This is not to say, however, that law reform is never used as an instrument for changing public opinion; if Parliament slavishly followed popular opinion we might still be hanging little children for petty theft.

Should we always obey the law?
This is essentially a moral question and a matter of line-drawing. We saw in the last section that some branches of the criminal law are taken more seriously than others; many motorists habitually break the law, some may even take pride in so doing. Many people who would be horrified to be branded as thieves habitually "fiddle" their tax returns or their claims for travel expenses.

Part of the answer to this question lies in weight of numbers. If enough people break the law then that law ceases to have more than a theoretical existence; though this does not answer the essentially moral question of whether such laws can *rightfully* be disobeyed. There would be very solid social as well as moral grounds for deploring a situation in which vast numbers of people had no respect for one another's property or where everyone reserved the right to decide whether they would drive on the righthand side or the lefthand side of the road. But certainly the law is difficult to enforce if it is widely disregarded and there is a danger that the agencies of law enforcement will make themselves ridiculous. There is currently a debate about whether this situation now exists with regard to laws prohibiting the use of "soft" drugs like cannabis.

In 1941 1,000 coal miners at the Betteshanger Colliery in Kent were prosecuted for striking in contravention of wartime laws. Special magistrates' hearings were arranged and the outcome was described by one witness in the following words:

Everything on the day was orderly and even festive. Bands played and women and children cheered the procession on its way to the Court. The proceedings in Court went smoothly; everyone pleaded guilty. The three Union officials were sent to prison. The Branch Secretary was sentenced to two months with hard labour; the local President and a member of the local executive each received one month with hard labour. Thirty-five men were fined £3 or one month's imprisonment, and nearly one thousand were fined £1, or fourteen days.[6]

The strike continued, and the authorities had to climb down. The men imprisoned were released. The Clerk of the Court reported that only nine of the men fined had paid up. It was quite obvious that the defaulters could not be imprisoned without further embarrassment to the court and to the government, so the fines were quietly forgotten.

In the early 1970s local authorities proclaimed their intention to defy government legislation abolishing free school milk and others defied the "fair rents" scheme laid down in the Housing Finance Act 1972 (see chapter 5). If the councils had stood together with Clay Cross then the government would have been forced into a position of having to decide whether to exercise default powers in every case, but most of the authorities wavered and eventually backed down.

Another instance was the noisy campaign of trade unionists against the Industrial Relations Act 1971, consisting, in part, of defiance of the powers of the now deceased Industrial Relations Court. In this context the chairman of the Labour Party's Tribune Group, Norman Atkinson MP, was reported as distinguishing in a speech between two kinds of law: "ordinary" law, which must be obeyed, and "political or ideological law", which "calls upon elected people [such as trade union officials or elected councillors] to implement it. In a democracy such law should never be enforced by threat of surcharge, fines or imprisonment"[7]. These distinctions seem wholly unreal. Every Act of Parliament passed in the face of opposition might be said to have a "political" content. Why should elected bodies be singled out for this kind of privileged treatment?

Nevertheless, civil disobedience, justified on the basis that some laws are so wicked that one has a positive duty to disobey them, has a long and respectable pedigree rooted in ideas about natural law.

Ultimately the correctness of particular acts of disobedience can be assessed only with the benefit of hindsight. People condemned now as agitators, cranks and even traitors may one day be hailed as heroes. Those Germans who defied Hitler's cruel laws were legally guilty of treason, but we see them now as men of high courage and honour.

Most people would agree, however, that disobedience of the law is not something to be used lightly. We all have a stake in an ordered society and we cannot pick and choose those bits of the law we agree with and disregard those we dislike. What we surely can and must do is see that laws are made and enforced rationally and with due regard to the interests of different groups in society.

There are usually plenty of ways of agitating for change or of showing disapproval without indulging in outright disobedience of the law; but there are some circumstances where civil disobedience may indeed be the last ditch against tyranny or the last hope of those who feel that their position has become so impossible that they have nothing to lose. There are numerous issues of private conscience (for example, the views of various religious groups about Sabbath observance or the propriety of undergoing medical treatment) for which the law can make no satisfactory provision, other than being flexible and sympathetic to particular cases. In a pluralist society where different and sometimes conflicting values are jumbled together, the law will inevitably cut across a lot of private susceptibilities.

The answer seems to be that if your conscience tells you to disobey the law then it is open to you to do so, at a price. It is no good breaking the law and then complaining when you are punished. People who do disobey the law on a matter of principle still owe some responsibility to those around them and to the state within which they live. Whatever their contemporaries may think, history will be the ultimate judge of their behaviour and of the law which they have elected to defy. And history can be a harsh judge.

3 Varieties and Sources of English Law

> Individuals or bodies legislating in subordination to the sovereign are more properly *reservoirs* fed from the source of all law, the supreme legislature, and again emitting the borrowed waters which they receive from that Fountain of Law.
>
> JOHN AUSTIN

One cannot go very far in studying law without coming across numerous subdivisions of the subject. There are important differences between, for example, civil law and criminal law, yet in some contexts these two categories seem to merge together in a bewildering way. The early history of English law is strewn with unseemly demarcation disputes between courts trying to filch lucrative jurisdictions from one another, often by the use of elaborate legal "fictions". Why has the law got so fragmented? Why is there not a large book called *English Law* to which we could refer for all our legal information?[1]

The precise answer to the first question could be found only by historical analysis, though modern characteristics of the law may bear little resemblance to what has gone before. For example, what lawyers call the rules of equity grew up through the practice of medieval Lord Chancellors ("keepers of the king's conscience") in providing alternative legal remedies, more flexible than those available in the ordinary courts of common law. Equity itself gradually became more and more rigid, a quite separate body of chancery courts grew up to administer it, and eventually it was fused with the common law by an Act passed in 1873. Although lawyers still talk about equity, and there is a Chancery Division of the High Court, equity is now almost indistinguishably woven into the fabric of English law.

Fig. 3.1 Principal categories of law

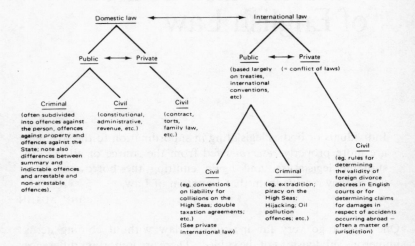

Note   Double arrow ◄─► indicates links between two categories eg. courts, rules, procedures
in common; precedents laid down in one context may be applicable in another, etc.
All the above categories can be further subdivided — eg.
1   by <u>source</u> eg. judge-made law (common law) or statute law
2   into <u>substantive</u> law (ie. the content of the rules of law in question) and
<u>adjectival</u> law (ie. the procedures which operate in respect of rules of substantive law)

International law

The main subdivisions of English law can be seen in fig. 3.1. One must first distinguish between domestic law and international law. Those who hold that the basic characteristic of law is the existence of a sovereign body with the capacity to enforce its rulings hesitate to include international law under the heading of law at all. Ultimately, obedience to international law rests much more on political expediency than on enforcement machinery.

Many international disputes can, in theory, be adjudicated by international bodies such as the International Court at the Hague, but the enforceability of such decisions depends on *political* circumstances – for example, on the respective diplomatic and military strengths of the parties, the economic and commercial relationships between them, and whether or not the issue is one where national governments want to make a virtue of abiding by the law or want to be seen to be taking a stand against the "meddling" of outsiders.

In the Icelandic fisheries dispute, in 1974, Iceland declined to recognise the jurisdiction of the International Court, even though she was a signatory to the original treaty setting it up; England has stood, rather uncertainly, on her "legal" rights. In different political circumstances (for example, if the people of Iceland had been divided in their views of their government's action or if the court's decision had been different) the boot might have been on the other foot. The most promising methods for resolving these kinds of disputes lie in the realms of diplomacy rather than of international law.

In at least one recent instance Britain herself has vacillated in her attitude towards an international legal institution. In 1950 the United Kingdom acted as one of the original signatories of the European Convention on Human Rights, set up under the auspices of the Council of Europe (not to be confused with the European Economic Community). The Convention is enforced principally through the European Commission of Human Rights (composed of distinguished jurists from the twenty-one member countries) and the European Court of Justice which sits at Strasbourg.

In 1966 Britain agreed, rather belatedly, to allow individual citizens to petition the Commission about alleged violations of their rights under the Convention, initially for a period of three years, subsequently extended for further periods of three years and two years respectively. The Government soon found itself on the defensive in one or two embarrassing cases, particularly in respect of petitions concerning Britain's treatment of the Kenyan Asians in the period following enactment of the Commonwealth Immigrants Act 1968, and other petitions alleging the use of torture by the security forces in Northern Ireland. Apart from the latter case, the European Court has held the United Kingdom to be in violation of the Convention in respect of prisoners' rights to consult their lawyer, birching of offenders in the Isle of Man and (in 1979) over the contempt of court ruling which prevented the *Sunday Times* from publishing an article on the drug, Thalidomide.

Some lawyers have argued that British law already provides adequate safeguards against violations of human rights, and since the end of 1973 there have been recurrent rumours that Britain would decline to renew the right of individuals to petition; the former Greek military regime is the only government to have taken this step up to now.[2] The matter has been further complicated by rulings of the EEC

Court, which take account of human rights aspects of Community Law: and all this is part of the debate about a UK Bill of Rights (see chapter 7).

International laws are currency in the game of international politics. Governments usually like to be able to bask in the public's awareness that the law is on their side; but it may sometimes be more expedient to deny the validity of such law. In the last analysis the effective working of all international institutions is dependent on the continuing goodwill of individual nations, witness the failure of the much vaunted League of Nations in the 1930s.

The principles underlying international law have a lot to do with "natural law". It is assumed that there are absolute standards of fair dealing and humane behaviour that all civilised men will recognise; nations may get drawn into the web of international law for fear of appearing uncivilised if they do not. The drawing up of lists of war crimes by the victors in the Second World War was based on the natural law notion that some kinds of behaviour are so outrageous that every rational and civilised person would agree on condemning them. It is a moot point, however, whether it was ever a meaningful exercise to impose Western Christian-Judaic standards of morality and justice on the alien culture of Japan. War crimes trials tend, in retrospect, to look a bit like judicialised lynchings.

Much international law, however, does not rest on natural law principles as such but consists of arrangements of mutual convenience between nations. Thus countries commonly make extradition treaties so that criminals from one territory cannot seek refuge by crossing national boundaries (offences of a "political" character are usually excluded so that *bona fide* refugees can obtain political asylum, though this gives rise to tricky problems of definition). There are international agreements about crimes of piracy and hijacking; about double taxation (so that citizens who spend part of their lives abroad do not have to pay tax on the same income to two separate governments); and about international trade and finance.

English law and the European Communities
A feature of treaties is that they often have to be incorporated into domestic law by Acts of Parliament. This provides Parliament with one of its few weapons for monitoring international affairs, though

the treaties themselves are negotiated in the privacy of diplomatic channels and Parliament has no real opportunity of rejecting or amending them and may not always be fully aware of the relevant circumstances. The most important single instance of this kind of treaty ratification in recent years was the enactment of the European Communities Act 1972, ratifying Britain's decision to sign the Treaty of Rome.

Many of the opponents of Britain's entry into the EEC have argued on the grounds that it constitutes a surrender of parliamentary sovereignty. It is arguable, however, that this is a matter of degree rather than of principle. Every treaty a nation signs and every international organisation it joins represents a voluntary surrender of a fraction of its autonomy, for which, of course, the government concerned hopes to get something of at least equal value in return.

Much of the controversy centres on the extent to which Community institutions can pass laws which have binding force in the United Kingdom. The Rome Treaty provides that certain kinds of Community law, mostly trivial and transitory regulations made by the Commission in relation to the Common Agricultural Policy, are effective without ratification by the Westminster Parliament. But the more important Community laws are available in draft long before they come into effect, are considered by the European Parliament (which contains a substantial British membership), and they often have to be incorporated into law by means of a statutory instrument which can, at least in theory, be debated and rejected by Parliament. Parliament certainly has heavy responsibilities in respect of our membership of the Communities and special machinery has been devised for scrutiny.[3]

The chronic incapacity of Parliament to monitor, still less to control, the Executive generally leads one to doubt whether "parliamentary sovereignty" is a very meaningful concept anyway, except in a rather abstract sense (see pp. 34–36).

Conflict of laws

International law is commonly subdivided into "public" and "private" elements, the latter being known as conflict of laws. Conflict of laws arises where, for example, there is some doubt about which country's legal system is relevant to a case; if two British servicemen are motoring in Malta, and collide with one another, can the injured party sue in the British courts where the rules relating to the award of damages are more generous than in Maltese law?[4] Clearly the line must be drawn somewhere; judges are very wary of a practice called "forum shopping" whereby a litigant tries to choose the legal system which he thinks will give him the best deal.

Problems in conflict of laws arise extensively in international trade and also in matters like divorce; is a polygamous marriage or a Muslim divorce recognisable under English law? Clearly the answer matters a lot when it affects things like the distribution of marital property or the rights of divorced parties to remarry. Sometimes the government will settle the matter by international agreement and/or by statute.

Public law and private law

There is an important division in domestic law between public and private law. Broadly speaking, private law comprises those areas of law involving private citizens, while public law is that area of law in which the state has a direct interest. Thus public law is generally taken to consist of administrative and constitutional law (see chapter 5); to this might be added revenue law and criminal law.

There remains some ambiguity. Most lawyers would regard an ordinary civil action (for example, for breach of contract) against a public authority as being in the realm of private rather than of public law because, although the state is party to the action, the law that applies in many such cases is identical to that which would apply in a similar action between two citizens, though special rules do apply to contracts made by the Crown and by corporate bodies. So it is necessary to amend the definition to take account of whether or not the involvement of the state is purely incidental to the form that the proceedings take.

Civil and criminal law

For most practical purposes, the most crucial distinction of all is between civil and criminal law. The following definitions suffice for most purposes but, as we shall see, they are far from watertight:

Civil law is that branch of law that deals with the legal relations between citizens. Civil proceedings involve a plaintiff suing a defendant in a civil court. A successful civil action most commonly results in the defendant paying damages to the plaintiff to compensate him for the loss he has actually suffered, though there are many other kinds of remedy such as "specific performance" (compelling the defendant to keep to his side of a bargain), a "declaration" of the plaintiff's legal rights, or some kind of matrimonial relief (a divorce decree, an order for maintenance, etc). To succeed, a plaintiff must prove his case on "a balance of probabilities".

Criminal law is that branch of the law by which the state regulates the conduct of its citizens. Criminal proceedings involve the prosecution of an accused person (or defendant) in a criminal court. The outcome of a successful prosecution is the conviction of the accused followed by the imposition of a criminal penalty upon him. Only the Crown can agree to such a penalty being remitted, whereas in civil proceedings it is open to the plaintiff to forgo the judgment in his favour. To succeed, the prosecution must prove its case "beyond reasonable doubt".

In all but a sprinkling of marginal cases there is no problem determining whether a case is civil or criminal, but here are some of the ways in which the boundary between the two categories is blurred:

1. Not all criminal proceedings are initiated by the state and not all civil proceedings are started by private citizens. The state can commence civil actions, and it can be sued; and there is a long-established facility for the private citizen to bring a private prosecution, though Parliament has laid down the requirement in some cases, as with prosecutions under the Official Secrets Acts, that prosecutions can be brought only with official leave. One famous private prosecution of recent years was Mr Francis Bennion's partly successful action in 1972 against Mr Peter Hain for disrupting sporting fixtures during the "Stop the 70 Tour" campaign against apartheid.

2. The distinction between civil and criminal courts is far from clear-cut (see chapter 4). For example, magistrates' courts have a civil as well as a criminal jurisdiction; and the higher appellate courts deal both with civil and with criminal matters.

3. Some actions can be both crimes and the subject of civil proceedings. If someone punches me on the nose I can sue him for damages for assault and battery in the civil courts and he may find himself prosecuted in the criminal courts for assault or, if he hits me hard

enough, causing grievous bodily harm. The same is true of causing malicious damage to property or causing death by dangerous driving; an employer who fails to fence his machinery in accordance with the Factories Acts can be prosecuted for a statutory offence and sued for breach of his statutory duty by someone who is injured in consequence.

It is not always the case, however, that criminal offences can give rise to civil actions. If a witness tells lies in criminal proceedings with the result that the person accused spends a long spell in prison before the lie is discovered, then the liar can be prosecuted for perjury; but the unfortunate victim cannot get civil damages for the loss he has suffered.[5]

4. It is an oversimplification to suggest that punishment is the inevitable sequel to criminal conviction and that the payment of compensation is confined to civil actions. Some of those convicted in the criminal courts are put on probation rather than being punished. The treatment of juvenile offenders has, especially in recent years, emphasised treatment and rehabilitation rather than punishment.

Until recently, persistent debt defaulters could be imprisoned by the civil courts; punishment can be inflicted for contempt of court in both civil and criminal proceedings. Criminal courts can in many cases order the payment of compensation by a convicted person. In limited circumstances the civil courts can add "punitive damages" to the amount the defendant would ordinarily pay the plaintiff to compensate him for his loss.

5. There may be a measure of cross-reference between civil and criminal proceedings. For example, section 11 of the Civil Evidence Act 1968 provides that a conviction in the criminal courts can be adduced in evidence in civil proceedings; before this, the civil courts trying an action for negligence against a motorist had to ignore the latter's earlier conviction for dangerous driving, even though the criminal proceedings had related to precisely the same incident.

The change arose following the activities of Mr Alfred Hinds who mounted a spectacular campaign (involving several escapes from prison) to prove his innocence following a conviction for his alleged part in a robbery. Mr Hinds successfully brought a libel action against the policeman who had prosecuted him and who was imprudent enough to write a newspaper article at a later date re-affirming Hinds's guilt.

The case greatly embarrassed the prosecuting authorities and, since the passage of the 1968 Act it has become much harder for convicted persons to re-open their cases in the civil courts. In theory, however, such a person should have a much tougher time proving his innocence in a civil court than in a criminal court. In the latter he need only instil "reasonable doubt" in the minds of the jury whereas in civil proceedings he must establish his case on a "balance of probabilities".

Types of civil law

Even after agreeing on a more or less workable distinction between civil and criminal law, we quickly discover further problems of classification; both these types of law contain numerous subspecies.

Two of the most important subcategories of civil law are *contract* (the law relating to legally enforceable agreements) and *tort* (the area of law concerned with civil wrongs). The former can be further subdivided into such areas as shipping contracts ("charterparties"), hire purchase, sale of goods, etc, each of which will have been the subject of at least one textbook of daunting dimensions. The law of tort includes negligence, nuisance, trespass (notice boards threatening that "trespassers will be *prosecuted*" are bluff, trespass belongs to the civil law) and defamation (libel and slander).

Contract and tort are related to one another; a trader who sells dangerous goods can be sued in negligence for injuries so caused and may also be held liable for a breach of a contractual duty to see that his goods are of merchantable quality.

Of course, these two categories, important though they are, by no means exhaust the civil law. There are whole specialisms in family law, revenue law, patents and copyrights, trade unions and administrative law, all of which have their own specialist practitioners, their own textbooks and law reports, and, in some cases, their own courts and tribunals.

Some areas of civil law (including much of contract and tort) rests largely upon common law (that is, it is judge-made); other areas (for example, family law) are founded in part on statutes enacted by Parliament but have, in some aspects at least, been heavily modified by judicial reinterpretation; others (such as revenue and rating law) are almost entirely the creature of statute.

Types of criminal law

Criminal law too is subdivided in various ways. Some textbooks try to classify crimes under three clearcut headings: crimes against the state (treason, breaches of public order, etc), crimes against the person (murder, rape, assault, etc) and offences against property (theft, malicious damage, etc). Many offences in fact cut across these categories. The hijacking of an aircraft, for example, may be an offence against the state, against the person and against property, and may violate both domestic and international laws. And it does not need a very fertile imagination to paint a scenario in which someone would end up being charged with burglary, causing grievous bodily harm, assaulting the police, infringing the Official Secrets Act and driving a car without insurance.

In addition to these substantive subdivisions of criminal law, there are important categories which relate to an accused person's rights with respect to the legal process. First there is an important distinction between *summary* and *indictable* offences. In general, the latter are serious crimes, triable before judge and jury in the Crown Court; the former are mostly lesser crimes (including most motoring offences) triable in magistrates' courts without a jury. To complicate matters, there are many "hybrid" offences, which can be tried either summarily or on indictment; moreover, most indictable offences (for example theft, an offence covering a multitude of sins of vastly differing gravity) can be tried summarily with the consent of the accused and in some cases a person accused of an offence which is normally tried summarily can elect instead to be tried by jury (for example, in cases where he could be sentenced to more than three months imprisonment).[6] The accused often has to weigh the advantages of getting things over with quickly before the magistrates against hazarding his luck before a jury.

Then there is the distinction between *arrestable* and *non-arrestable* offences, established by the Criminal Law Act 1967 and superseding the age-old distinction between felonies and misdemeanours. Arrestable offences are ones in which the sentence is fixed by law or for which a person, not previously convicted, could be sent to prison for five years or more; anyone suspected of committing or of being about to commit one of these offences can be arrested without a warrant. Powers of arrest in respect of non-arrestable offences are generally more restricted.[7]

Adjectival and substantive law
Reference is sometimes made to *adjectival* as opposed to *substantive* law. The latter comprises the rules that actually make up the law (the law of murder, the law of contract, etc). But of at least equal importance are the adjectival rules which relate to the application of substantive law in real life, such as the rules of evidence, court procedure, costs and the ways of starting various kinds of legal action.

There is an old saying that justice under the English common law is "secreted in the interstices of procedure". It is no good having an impregnable case if your solicitor fails to tell you that the time limit within which your action has to be brought to court has just expired; it is no good relying on a witness whose testimony will be ruled out by the rules forbidding hearsay evidence. Far from being the poor relation of substantive law, adjectival law is the pith and marrow of procedural and substantive justice.

Another important criterion by which laws are subclassified is by their source. In particular, it may be important to consider whether a law derives from judicial precedent or from statute. This will be discussed in the sections that follow.

Common law and statute law
England is often said to be a common law country, in contrast to the codified systems of law prevailing on the Continent or the Roman-Dutch systems to be found, for example, in South Africa, and to the civilian-based jurisprudence of Scotland. In *Learning the Law*, Professor Glanville Williams suggests that the most usual meaning of the phrase common law is, "the law that is not legislation, that is, the law created by the custom of the people and the decisions of the judges". Hereafter the term will be taken as synonymous with judge-made law based on precedent.

Although English law has its main roots in common law blended with the old rules of equity, much of contemporary law is enshrined in Acts of Parliament and in delegated legislation. Law is the product of a complex interaction between the courts and Parliament. Thus in areas where Parliament has been active in passing legislation it has paid due regard to the common law already in existence, though this is not to say that judicial wisdom is accepted uncritically by legislators; some Acts may be intended to clear up a mess that the common law has got into. For their part, the judges do not shape the common law in isolation from the legal rules emanating from Parliament.

The quantity of statute law has increased at an enormous rate throughout this century. According to Professor Crick, the total number of pages in public Acts passed in 1900 was 198, in 1920 it was 560, in 1957 it was 1,103 and in 1964 it was 2,961, though the number of Acts passed annually (between about fifty and eighty) has not varied much.[8] By January 1974 there were 3,480 public general Acts on the Statute Book. There has also been a steady growth in the use of delegated legislation, issued under the authority of Acts of Parliament, to a point where the parliamentary machine for monitoring it has begun to creak very noisily indeed.

The courts and "parliamentary sovereignty"

It is often said that Parliament is "sovereign" in the law-making process, meaning, in effect, that its legislative powers are unlimited. This is a distorted view. For one thing, while it is true that all statute law emanates directly or indirectly from Parliament, the actual control which Parliament as a body exercises over the passage of legislation and the scope that it has for initiating legislative proposals and monitoring Acts after they are passed, is very limited.

In general there is a convention that a Parliament cannot bind its successors; but there have been some significant exceptions. The Act of Union with Scotland contains provisions which purport to safeguard the status of the Scottish Presbyterian Church against future amendment. The Statute of Westminster 1931, and subsequent enactments relating to the independent Commonwealth countries, deprives Parliament of the right to legislate on behalf of such countries. The European Communities Act 1972 compromises Parliament's unqualified power to pass laws at variance with Community law. The problem of "entrenched clauses" (statutory provisions that cannot be repealed or amended save by special legislative procedures) might arise if Britain ever enacted a Bill of Rights.

Nevertheless, for most practical purposes, the power of Parliament to enact laws is unqualified. But calling this "sovereignty" is not very helpful. The legislative powers of Parliament and the relationship of the latter to other institutions derives not from anything resembling immutable "laws of the constitution" but from time-honoured convention. The functions and powers of Parliament have changed out of all recognition over the centuries and the concept of sovereignty implies a permanency of function and importance which does not really accord with the present position.

The term "legislative sovereignty" is a shorthand way of saying that legislation which has undergone recognised processes in Parliament is generally treated by the courts as binding. There have been several unsuccessful attempts in recent years to persuade the courts to declare legislation invalid. This is an almost impossible task in a country which has no Bill of Rights and no written constitution giving the judiciary a special function of pronouncing on the constitutional propriety of Executive actions.

In 1967 Colin Jordan, self-styled leader of the British Nazi Party, was imprisoned for offences under the Race Relations Act 1965. He subsequently sought a writ of *habeas corpus* to secure his release, arguing that the 1965 Act contravened fundamental rights of free speech; but the judges held that they had no power to challenge legislation.[9] In another case a taxpayer disputed his tax liability on the grounds that some of the money would be spent on nuclear armaments in contravention of a Geneva Convention ratified by the British Government. But Mr Justice Ungoed-Thomas said:

What the statute itself enacts cannot be unlawful, because [it] is the highest form of law known to this country. It is the law which prevails over every other form of law, and it is not for the court to say that a parliamentary enactment . . . is unlawful.[10]

Challenges to the validity of delegated legislation are more likely to succeed, though even here the judges tread very warily. Successful challengers must show that the legislation is *ultra vires*, that is beyond the scope of the powers originally delegated by Parliament, and not that Parliament was wrong to have conferred those powers.

Although the courts recognise the power of Parliament to legislate in any manner it chooses, it is clear that in practice statute law cannot possibly cover every possible contingency, and often the meaning of a statute is open to more than one interpretation. (If this were not so lawyers would be deprived of a large portion of their business.) It is the judges who must apply statutes, intended to be of general application, to particular situations and to plug any gaps in them.

Until relatively recently, English judges adhered rigidly to the fiction that their task was simply to *apply* the laws enacted by Parliament and embodied in precedent; but nowadays more and more judges are willing to acknowledge the fact that their task of interpreting, adapting and sometimes repairing Parliament's work- manship is a creative one, that legislation is a complex process in which Parliament and the courts play mutually complementary roles. But at the same time, judges are inclined to camouflage their law-making role – which often means using rather tortuous rational- isations to manoeuvre around awkward precedents and statutes.

The clarity of the law

It is a well-known axiom of English law that "ignorance is no excuse". John Selden justified the existence of this principle as follows: "Ignorance of the law excuses no man; not that all men know the law, but because 'tis an excuse every man will plead, and no man can tell how to confute him."[11] Yet it has long been a matter for complaint that much of the law is unintelligible to the layman, and sometimes to the lawyer; few would agree with Lord Diplock's cynical assertion that the beauty of the common law is that "it is a maze and not a motorway".[12]

Much of the Statute Book is a muddle. As Lord Scarman has said:

> Under the guidance and with the paper provided by [the Statutory Publications] Office you . . . may insert into your collection of statutes, written amendments, text cancellations, and gummed slips of paper as additions to the text. The resultant mess has to be seen to be believed.[13]

Moreover, the verbal clarity of individual statutes often leaves much to be desired. Of the Rent and Mortgage Restrictions Acts, Lord Justice Mackinnon said:

> Having once more groped my way around that chaos of verbal darkness, I have come to the conclusion, with all becoming diffi- dence, that the county court judge was wrong in this case. My diffidence is increased by finding that my brother Luxmoore has groped his way to the contrary conclusion.[14]

If a senior appellate judge is baffled, what hope is there for the untutored layman? Every statute-user will have his own personal favourite in the obscurity stakes; as good a candidate as any is the statutory instrument picked out by the *Guinness Book of Records:*

> In the Nuts (Unground) (Other Than Ground Nuts) Order, the expression nuts shall have reference to such nuts, other than ground nuts, as would but for this amending Order not qualify as nuts (unground) (other than ground nuts) by reason of their being nuts (unground).

It has been suggested, not implausibly, that at least part of the problem lies in the need for a legislative instrument to satisfy two quite different audiences; first, Parliament, mostly composed of non-lawyers, which wants information about the general effect of each clause, and second, professional lawyers for whom the Act must provide a specific answer to a specific problem: "One customer wants a picture and the other wants a Bradshaw."[15] There is a tendency for Acts to fall between two stools and to end up by satisfying no one.

Many lawyers are very concerned about this problem. The Law Commission is permanently preoccupied with the Gargantuan task of promoting clarity in the law; and there is an influential lawyers' pressure group called the Statute Law Society which has produced reports on the subject.

Codification and consolidation: the Law Commission
One of the remedies for the deficiencies of the law is selective codification and consolidation. The former term has two meanings. The first is that the entire body of a country's law is stated in a single document; thus the law of France is set out in the *Code Napoléon*, promulgated in 1804. Such a sweeping change is hardly practicable save in times of revolutionary upheaval. The second meaning is the more modest process of gathering together statutory provisions and common law principles on a particular subject and incorporating them, with appropriate amendment, into a single enactment.

There has already been a small amount of codification in this country, very much on an *ad hoc* basis. Thus the Bills of Exchange Act 1882 incorporated some 2,500 cases and 17 statutes in a measure containing 100 sections. Other important instances are the Sale of Goods Act 1893 and the Theft Act 1968.

A more modest variant of codification is consolidation, which entails bringing together a number of related statutes (not precedents), cutting out what has already been repealed, making minor amendments, and fashioning the result into a tidy and compact Consolidation Act. There is a special parliamentary Joint Committee on Consolidation Bills, chaired by a Law Lord, which undertakes the scrutiny of such measures. The number of consolidation Bills enacted annually in recent years has averaged about ten.

It should be emphasised that codification and consolidation, while useful in tidying up the law, are not devices for achieving instant intelligibility. And even a comprehensive code on the Continental pattern is only appropriate at one point in time: as the years go by the most carefully formulated code will become defaced by judicial reinterpretation and "gummed slips of paper".

The whole process of tidying up the law, and reforming it, has been rationalised by the establishment of the Law Commission in 1965. The five-man Commission, plus a separate body for Scotland, is chaired by a High Court judge and has the task of devising law reform programmes, of examining specific areas of law and making proposals for reform, usually accompanied by a draft Bill, and of preparing programmes for the consolidation and revision of statute law.

The Law Commission has a symbolic function over and above its usefulness in tidying up the law, for it symptomises a healthy interest in law reform. Its establishment has taken at least some of the steam out of the case for a ministry of justice (see pp. 11–13).

Already the two Commissions have produced numerous reports and working papers.[16] Some of their draft Bills have been snapped up by backbench MPs seeking suitable subject matter for Private Members' Bills; not only are such Bills often favoured by the government and therefore quite likely to succeed, but also the Member has no need to worry about the trouble and expense of getting the measure properly drafted.

It should be noted that the Law Commissions are not the only standing bodies concerned with law reform. Since 1959 there has been a Criminal Law Revision Committee to which the Home Secretary periodically refers criminal-legal problems (this body was responsible for the Theft Act 1968, and we shall encounter its most controversial report in chapter 7). The Lord Chancellor has at his disposal the Statute Law Committee, most of whose functions have passed to the Law Commission, the Law Reform Committee, concerned mostly with revising common law, and the Committee on Private International Law (that is, conflict of laws – see p. 28).

In addition, there have, over the years, been innumerable departmental committees and royal commissions to look at particular aspects of law and the machinery of justice. There are numerous unofficial bodies like *Justice* (the British section of the International Commission of Jurists); the Society of Labour Lawyers; the Inns of Court Conservative and Unionist Association; and the Statute Law Society, all of which have served to maintain informed debate about law reform. Most pressure groups devote at least part of their energy to monitoring the law in their particular field and agitating for change; bodies like the RSPCA, the motoring organisations, the Consumers' Association and the Lord's Day Observance Society have all played a part in advancing (or retarding – it depends on where the commentator happens to be standing) the progress of particular aspects of reform.

So, there is no shortage of inspiration for law reform, though it is a moot point whether the bodies which work in this area do much to encroach on the "Establishment's" domination of the law-making process. The Law Commission is composed of senior lawyers; there is a tendency for those who make the significant decisions in pressure groups to be isolated from the rank and file membership. But at least the debate about reform is taking place and part of it in public. What is still lacking is a coherent means for gathering the threads together, which brings us back to the idea for a ministry of justice.

Judges and the interpretation of statutes
It has already been hinted that judges have some leeway in interpreting the laws enacted by Parliament. Some statutes are ambiguous in their meaning; some may be an affront to a judge's idea of substantive justice or commonsense. What can the judge do about it?-

The safest course he can adopt is to take refuge in the view that Parliament knows best and that the court can only take the words of a statute at their face-value, however absurd the outcome. But some judges argue that, in such cases, it is open to the court to repair the deficiency. The most famous modern exposition of this view is by Lord Denning (Master of the Rolls since 1962):

The English language is not an instrument of mathematical precision. Our literature would be much the poorer if it were.

This is where the draftsmen of Acts of Parliament have often been unfairly criticised. . . . It would certainly save the judges trouble if Acts of Parliament were drafted with divine prescience and perfect clarity. In the absence of it, when a defect appears a judge cannot simply fold his hands and blame the draftsman. He must set to work on the constructive task of finding the intention of Parliament. . . . Put into homely metaphor [the principle to be followed is this: A judge should ask himself the question: If the makers of the Act had themselves come across this ruck in the texture of it, how would they have straightened it out? A judge must not alter the material of which it is woven, but he can and should iron out the creases.[17]

This assertion of the creative role of judges found little favour with Viscount Simonds who, in a later case, said this of Lord Denning's advice:

It appears to me to be a naked usurpation of the legislative function under the thin guise of interpretation. And it is the less justifiable when it is guesswork with what material the legislature would, if it had discovered the gap, have filled it in. If a gap is disclosed, the remedy lies in an amending Act.[18]

The issue is one of temperament rather than of general principle. Some judges are more willing than others to acknowledge a "creative" role in respect of statutes (and indeed in respect of precedents). Lord Denning goes further than most; but even Viscount Simonds was not above exercising his creative faculties on occasions when it suited his purpose. This is another illustration of the perennial problem of what is to be done when pursuit of due process and legalistic values conflicts with the attainment of substantive justice.

The doctrine of precedent
Common law is founded on a doctrine of precedent (sometimes called *stare decisis*). The emphasis on precedent in English law is much more marked than in other legal systems like those on the Continent, in the United States (even though, historically its legal system is rooted in English common law) and in Scotland.
    The rules about precedent are complicated, but the main principles are readily discernible. The first ingredient is a hierarchy of courts

(something we shall examine in more detail in the next chapter), the principles of law laid down by "superior" courts must be accepted as binding on all courts of inferior jurisdiction (and sometimes on the superior court itself) in later cases. Thus a precedent established by the House of Lords binds the Court of Appeal and the High Court;[19] decisions of the Court of Appeal are binding on the High Court and, save in exceptional circumstances, on the Court of Appeal itself.[20] Magistrates' courts and county courts are bound by precedents established in the High Court and above. High Court judges are not absolutely bound by the rulings of other High Court judges, but they are expected (if only in courtesy) to give good reasons for departing from such precedents. Precedent is treated in a slightly more flexible way in the criminal courts where judges are, or should be, concerned more with substantive justice than with points of law.

It must be emphasised that the rules of precedent apply only to rulings on points of law; no two cases can possibly be the same on their facts. Sometimes, however, the law is interwoven with the facts. It is a question of *fact* whether a motorist has a given quantity of alcohol in his bloodstream; but it is a question of *law* whether that quantity is sufficient to secure his conviction under the statutory breathalyser laws. In a civil case it is a question of *fact* to determine the general character of a Water Board's pumping station (how many people work there, the nature of the work they do, etc) but it is a matter of legal inference from those facts, and probably a matter of applying precedent, whether a pumping station is a "factory" within the meaning of the Factories Acts.

Moreover, the principle of law on which a precedent is based must be essential to the decision in hand; this core of essential legal principle is called the *ratio decidendi* of the case. Judges, in giving their judgments, sometimes make observations about the law which are extraneous to the decision in hand; such statements are said to be *obiter dicta* (said in passing) and are not binding as precedents, though they may be listened to with respect in later cases.

The doctrine of precedent epitomises what Shklar calls legalism, a belief in certainty and rule-following (see p. 4). Certainly there is a great deal to be said for encouraging such characteristics in the judicial process. There is, however, a danger of inflexibility if precedent is followed too slavishly. Social conditions may change; even the most distinguished judges make mistakes. It would be absurd if no escape could be found from the mistakes of the past or if our law had to be a mummified corpse of long-dead social values.

There are devices by which the strict application of precedent can be softened; but, as is the case with statutory interpretation, the effectiveness of these devices depends very much upon the outlook of individual judges. There are circumstances in which a judge can disregard a precedent; for example, if faced with two conflicting precedents a judge may have to choose between them. If the circumstances of the case before the judge are materially different from those of an alleged precedent, then he can distinguish between them; "distinguishing" cases is a fine art which gives considerable scope to a judge who is determined to escape from the shackles of an awkward precedent, though some judges are more enterprising (some might call them less responsible) in this respect than others.

The best approach to precedent is, as in so many things, a middle course. It is probably a good idea for judges to adhere to precedent, but to be willing to soften its application in appropriate cases.

Law reports

It is no use having a doctrine of precedent without having, at the same time, a proper record of judicial decisions. Alongside the modern doctrine of precedent has grown up a complicated system of law reports containing the full text of important judgments, embellished with editorial summaries of what the case is about and what rule of law it is founded upon (the headnote) and, in some reports, a summary of the legal argument presented to the court.

It comes as a surprise to those unfamiliar with the law to discover how many different series of law reports there are. Some report important cases on all manner of subjects; others specialise in particular subjects such as revenue law, patent law or local government law. It may come as more of a surprise to discover that, despite the wide range of different reports, only a tiny fraction of the cases decided by the courts are reported; most cases in the House of Lords get into at least one series of reports, but this is only to be expected because, to get to the House of Lords, a case has to involve an important point of law. But in the Court of Appeal (civil division) only about 30 per cent of cases get into the main series of reports and in the High Court the proportion is probably more of the order of

1 per cent. Cases in crown courts, county courts and magistrates' courts are seldom, if ever, reported.

The reason for this is clear. The number of cases is enormous; most of them, particularly those in the lower courts, involve no novel point of law at all. So the law reports concentrate on publishing cases which set new precedents or raise important and novel points of law or procedure which are of practical interest to the legal practitioner. This process of selection places considerable responsibility on the shoulders of law reporters and editors but, despite its slightly ramshackle appearance, the law reporting system seems to work reasonably well. From time to time, however, there are complaints that an important case has been missed.

Reports are the lawyer's basic stock in trade; their accumulated bulk over the years is enormous. One cannot help wondering whether it is not beyond the wit of man to find ways of storing all this material (and statutes too) in a computer, with facilities for instant recall in lawyers' offices and in courtrooms throughout the country. No doubt this will eventually come about, though there is not much movement in that direction at present. (A note on how to look up law reports is provided as an appendix to this book.)

Judge-made law: the snail in the bottle
We have at several points encountered the proposition that judges share the task of making law with Parliament. Seldom are they called upon to conjure up new legal principles from nothing; they proceed mainly by fractionally extending the scope of a precedent that is already well established or by reinterpreting statutes.

One of the most famous cases of judicial law-making was a Scottish case in the House of Lords, *Donoghue* v *Stevenson*,[21] from which the modern English tort of negligence is derived.

Mrs Donoghue went with a friend to a café where they bought some ginger beer in a bottle made of opaque glass; she poured some out and drank it. The rest of the ginger beer was then poured out – and out floated the corpse of a long-dead snail. Revolted by the thought of what she had consumed, Mrs Donoghue went into a state of shock and also had a bad gastric upset. Could she get damages?

She could not sue the café proprietor because he could hardly have been expected to see through the opaque walls of a bottle;

and it was clear that he had bought the bottle on trust from the manufacturer. Mrs Donoghue had no contract with the manufacturer, but did the latter owe a legal duty to an ultimate consumer of his products? The precedents were confusing, and apparently in conflict, but a majority of the House of Lords managed to distil out of them a general proposition of law to cover the case. There follows an extract, from the judgment of Lord Atkin, explaining the scope of the manufacturer's duty of care:

> The liability for negligence . . . is no doubt based upon a general public sentiment of moral wrongdoing for which the offender must pay. But acts or omissions which any moral code would censure cannot in a practical world be treated so as to give a right to every person injured by them to demand relief. . . . The rule that you are to love your neighbour becomes in law, you must not injure your neighbour; and the lawyer's question, Who is my neighbour? receives a restricted reply. You must take reasonable care to avoid acts or omissions which you can reasonably foresee would be likely to injure your neighbour. Who, then, in law is my neighbour? The answer seems to be – persons who are so closely and directly affected by my act that I ought reasonably to have them in contemplation as being so affected when I am directing my mind to the acts or omissions which are called in question.

The main significance of *Donoghue* v *Stevenson* lies in the fact that the Law Lords chose to move the law forward rather than to let it remain in a state of confusion. Lord Macmillan, in his judgment, said that "the categories of negligence are never closed". From the relatively narrow proposition laid down in this case (that a duty of care is owed by the manufacturer of the chattels to the eventual user) the courts have derived the inspiration to extend the law of negligence into a wide range of different situations.

Negligence today does not merely apply to manufacturers of goods but also to the repairers of goods; not just to food and drink but also to items like clothing (such as one painful case where the manufacturer of underwear left them impregnated with an irritant chemical), motor cars, etc; it covers the defective labelling of goods. It can even provide a remedy where someone has suffered loss as a result of receiving inaccurate professional advice.

This is a classic instance of an area of the common law which has been developed without parliamentary intervention, and without any of the successive steps taken in the process of development being really radical departures from what has gone before. The judicial process can change the law quite radically, but it tends to move by stealth rather than by frontal assault. It is an excellent example of what modern students of decision-making would call "incrementalism".

4 Courts and Lawyers

The first thing we do, let's kill all the lawyers.

WILLIAM SHAKESPEARE, *Henry VI, Part II*

A broad doorway leads into a fake-medieval hall, like a stripped-down cathedral, adorned with big black-letter notices announcing "Lord Chief Justice's Court", or "Wash and Brush Up". Dark-suited men carrying blue or red bags walk into a room by the entrance, and emerge a few minutes later solemnly wearing gowns, tabs and horse-hair or nylon wigs.

ANTHONY SAMPSON, describing the Royal Courts of Justice

We have spent some time examining the relationship between law and politics and have established that legal and political processes are tightly interwoven. In order to understand the nature of the relationship it is necessary to look at the processes of legislation and adjudication in given systems. It is important too to look at institutional arrangements, for these reflect certain characteristics of the state itself.

There are, for example, historical reasons why the United States has a written constitution and a Supreme Court empowered to challenge the constitutional propriety of legislation; Britain has no written constitution and no such Supreme Court. There are clear reasons why federal systems of government have more complex and overlapping court structures than unitary systems; Britain is, for the time being, a unitary state, but there is a distinctive legal system in Scotland (linked to that of England through appeals to the House of Lords and through legislative enactments applying in common to both countries). Moreover, the Judicial Committee of the Privy

Council, sitting in London, exercises an appellate jurisdiction in respect of a number of Commonwealth countries.

To some extent, as we have seen, British government is organised on the basis of a fiction of separation of powers. Countries like the Soviet Union maintain no such fiction; little secret is made of the fact that the courts are instruments for the enforcement both of law and the total ideology incorporated into that law. The idea of "administrative justice" enforced by an independent judiciary would be completely alien to the Soviet system. So examination of characteristics like judicial independence, the manner in which lawyers are recruited and how they organise their professional arrangements, and the structure of a country's system of courts and tribunals, can reveal a lot about the governmental process in that country.

This chapter is not intended as a guide book to the courts; such books are available elsewhere (see Bibliography). But for quick reference, the main features of the court system are shown in fig. 4.1.

Such a two dimensional plan can only be an oversimplification. For example, the central broken vertical line signifies the division between courts exercising civil and criminal jurisdictions respectively; but, as we saw in chapter 3, the distinction is not altogether clearcut. The hierarchical character of the system (see p. 41) has been indicated by putting "superior" courts at the top of the diagram and "inferior" ones at the bottom. In practice, however, the hierarchy is less well defined. In some respects the Court of Appeal is "superior" (that is, for the purposes of setting binding precedents) to the Divisional Courts of the High Court; but on the criminal side the appellate jurisdiction of the Queen's Bench Divisional Court is in parallel rather than in series with the jurisdiction exercised by the criminal division of the Court of Appeal. For convenience, the Judicial Committee of the Privy Council appears at the top of the diagram and tribunals are placed at the bottom, though neither is really a part of the ordinary hierarchy of courts at all.

Some recent changes

In the 1870s there was a major overhaul of the machinery of justice, resulting in the establishment of the High Court and the civil Court of Appeal in much the same form in which they exist today; at the same time, the position of the House of Lords as the final court of appeal was rationalised (up to that point it had been threatened with

Fig. 4.1 Outline of English court structure

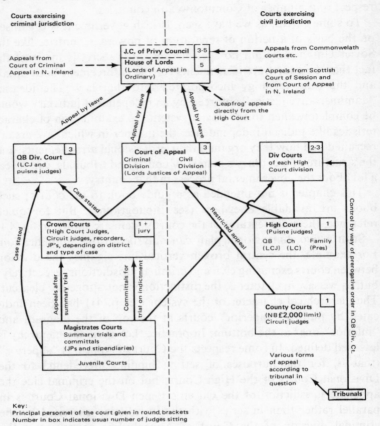

Key:
Principal personnel of the court given in round brackets
Number in box indicates usual number of judges sitting

extinction). The last decade or so has seen further changes of comparable magnitude, perhaps symptomising a fashionable political interest in issues of law reform.

Fig. 4.1 shows the position as it is in the early 1980s; as little as twenty years ago the picture would have been very different. In 1966, for example, the Court of Criminal Appeal (set up in 1907) was replaced by a criminal division of the Court of Appeal, the latter having been, up to that time, exclusively a civil court. In 1970 the High Court was reorganised. For historical reasons, the Court had, since 1882, been divided into three divisions, Queen's Bench, Chancery and Probate,

Divorce and Admiralty (PDA). The latter had a rather curious mixture of business, summed up by the late Sir Alan Herbert as "wills, wives and wrecks". The distribution of jurisdictions, particularly in the area of family law, was anomalous; so the Administration of Justice Act 1970 set up a new Family Division in place of the PDA, and gave the latter's probate jurisdiction to the Chancery Division and its admiralty jurisdiction to the Queen's Bench Division. In 1971 a brand new court was added to the structure, in the shape of the National Industrial Relations Court, but subtracted again in 1974.

The Beeching Report

In 1967 the Royal Commission on Assizes and Quarter Sessions was set up under the chairmanship of Lord Beeching (formerly chairman of British Rail) to deal with what was felt to be a mounting crisis in the operation of the judicial machine.

The Report of the Royal Commission concluded that:

> It stands out clearly from any survey of the pattern of criminal and civil courts that the system was devised for circumstances which no longer exist and that, in spite of the very great changes in the life of the country, in the distribution of population, in the mobility of people, and in national and local government, far too much has been retained only because it is traditional.[1]

Increased pressure of court business, particularly in London, resulted in people often having to wait months for their trial to take place; this pressure had been exacerbated by the increasing availability of legal aid in both civil and criminal proceedings. The assize system, whereby High Court judges went on circuit to the provinces to try important civil and criminal cases, dated back to the thirteenth century, and had hardly changed since; towns like Coventry and Hull had no assize courts, but there were fifteen assize towns with populations under 10,000 and three of these had fewer than 1,500. Courts of quarter sessions, dealing with all but the most serious criminal cases and hearing appeals from magistrates' courts, were also distributed in an anomalous manner; moreover, they had become too dependent on part-time judges. Civil business in assize courts had always suffered because of the priority given to criminal trials.

The main recommendations of the Royal Commission were as follows:

1. All the higher criminal courts (assizes, quarter sessions, the Central Criminal Court in London, and the Crown Courts of Manchester and Liverpool) should be abolished and replaced by a new system of crown courts. The latter would be staffed by a new kind of full-time judge, circuit judges (who are also county court judges) assisted where necessary by part-time judges called recorders; High Court judges would continue to visit some crown courts to try serious crimes (see (3)). (The Central Criminal Court – otherwise called the Old Bailey – has in fact survived the Beeching axe.)

2. On the civil side, High Court civil business should be kept quite separate from criminal business, and be concentrated in only a few crown court centres. In suitable cases, High Court judges should be empowered to release cases normally triable only by them for trial by circuit judges. County courts should be kept separate from the High Court, be presided over by circuit judges, and have their ordinary jurisdiction increased from £500 to £1,000.

3. A majority of the Royal Commission considered that solicitors as well as barristers should be eligible for appointment as circuit judges and recorders (see below).

4. For purposes of court administration, the country should be divided into six circuits, each presided over by a High Court judge and organised by a professional circuit administrator. In rationalising the distribution of courts, nineteen assize towns and sixty-seven towns with courts of quarter sessions should be stripped of criminal courts above the level of magistrates; crown courts in fourteen former assize towns would no longer be visited by a High Court judge to try serious crime. (The result of this reorganisation can be seen on the map, fig. 4.2.)

5. The Lord Chancellor should become the minister solely responsible for administering all higher courts and county courts, as well as assuming responsibility for court buildings (formerly some of these functions had been shared with the Home Office and with local government).

6. For the purpose of distributing criminal business between different crown courts (some of which would be visited by High Court judges, others not) offences should be "banded". Some crimes should be triable only by a High Court judge; others should normally be tried by a High Court judge unless he released it from

Fig. 4.2

CIRCUITS: HIGH COURT AND CROWN COURT CENTRES FOR ENGLAND AND WALES

Source. Britain 1973, HMSO.

his list; a third category (covering most offences) would be triable by any category of criminal judge.

7. Crown courts would take over the jurisdiction of quarter sessions to hear appeals from magistrates' courts and, for that purpose, should consist of circuit judges, with magistrates exercising the role of assessors (sitting with the judge as non-voting members of the court) – see below.

The Beeching Report was published in September 1969; it was a crisp and ·sensible document, which was promptly acted on by the government. Indeed, before it appeared, the Administration of Justice Act 1969 raised the jurisdiction of county courts to £750 (it has since become £2,000, and proposals were published in September 1980 to raise this to £5,000). The Administration of Justice Act 1970 empowered the Lord Chancellor to dispense with assize courts in appropriate places. Even before the publication of the Courts Bill, implementing the main recommendations, an active search had begun for new court buildings and for administrative staff.

The Courts Act 1971

The Courts Bill came before Parliament in the session 1970–71 and, thanks to the foundations already laid, was brought into effect as early as January 1972. It followed the main lines of Beeching, leaving such matters as the location of courts and details of "banding" to be arranged by administrative directive.

Table 4.1 The six circuits: summary

Circuit	Location of main administrative office	Number of circuit judges (1980)
Midland and Oxford	Birmingham	37
Northern	Salford	37
North Eastern	Leeds	31
South Eastern	London	145
Wales and Chester	Cardiff	17
Western	Bristol	28

It departed from Beeching in two important respects. First, it provided for magistrates to sit as fully-fledged judges alongside circuit judges on appeals in the Crown Court (magistrates had expressed annoyance about their relegation to the role of assessors). Second, it rejected the majority proposal that solicitors should be eligible for appointment as circuit judges and recorders (see below). In addition, it made one or two changes which had not been part of the Beeching plan – in particular, the introduction of majority verdicts in civil trials by jury.

The Bill was welcomed on all sides, but the proposal to debar solicitors from judicial appointments sparked off a controversy which showed the legal profession in rather a poor light. Barristers (as we shall see later in this chapter) have always regarded the Bench as their own exclusive preserve. The squabble between the two branches of the profession reached such a pitch that the Lord Chancellor was forced to call the two sides together for joint consultations. A compromise was announced whereby solicitors could become judges, but only by instalments. Barristers *or* solicitors of ten years' standing in their professions could become recorders (part-time judges), and recorders of five years standing could become circuit judges.

The Beeching reforms have certainly improved the processes of administering the criminal courts and have swept away many of the archaisms and anomalies associated with the old system of assizes and quarter sessions. But, as the old phrase has it, "justice delayed is justice denied", and the delays in bringing cases to trial have remained, as those responsible for administering the courts admit, a very serious problem. In answer to a parliamentary question on 13 November 1978, the then Solicitor General, Mr Peter Archer, expressed deep concern at the average waiting time for trials in crown courts. This had risen from a bad 11·2 weeks in 1972 to a worse 13·7 weeks by June 1978; in London it averaged an appalling 25·2 weeks. (The figures are broken down in more detail in the annual *Judicial Statistics*.) Mr Archer mentioned substantial plans for new court buildings. One contributory factor has been the unsatisfactory distribution of criminal business between crown courts and magistrates' courts, a problem discussed, but not solved, in the James Report of 1975 (see chapter 3, note 6). It must always be remembered that recurrent political clamour for "law and order" involves a high cost, not just in terms of extra public money having to be spent (itself a vexed issue nowadays), but also in terms of the stress imposed upon a creaking judicial system (and, of course, on the police).

Thus the reforms are welcome as far as they go, but some defects are inherent in the system. We still have the same cumbersome trial process, based on juries (in criminal trials at least) and oral evidence. And calling criminal courts "crown courts" has not eliminated the range of different jurisdictions among them. We have not fully eliminated the two problems of judges having to move from one court to another and of the use of part-time judges, both of which mean that it is so often necessary to shuffle the list of cases (at inconvenience to the parties) to make optimum use of scarce judicial time.

Magistrates' courts

The system of criminal justice in Britain rests heavily on the role of lay magistrates (justices of the peace); and magistrates' courts were left untouched by the Beeching reforms. As one commentator points out:

> Every year . . . one in every forty persons in this country will appear before the magistrates. Of the cases heard in the courts 97·5 per cent are dealt with by the lay magistracy. . . . The only contact with justice for a massive proportion of the population will be with these amateur judges.[2]

Even the figure of 97·5 per cent understates the work done by these courts since *every* criminal case has to start in them; cases tried on indictment in the Crown Court begin with committal proceedings before magistrates, who have to satisfy themselves that the case against the accused is strong enough to warrant his being sent for trial. This duplication of proceedings was streamlined by the Criminal Justice Act 1967, which provided for nearly all committal proceedings to be conducted on the basis of documentary rather than oral evidence. Magistrates also have an important civil jurisdiction, particularly in the fields of family law (for example, for maintenance orders); and there is a separate juvenile bench.

The great strength of magistrates' courts is also their main weakness. They are very quick, but, bearing in mind the need for justice to be *seen* to be done, there is something almost indecent in the speed with which cases are disposed of; even an occasional plea of "not guilty" acts only as a temporary brake on the rapidly moving procession of defendants through the court. These courts do not state the legal reasoning underlying their decisions (though they can be asked to "state a case" on a point of law for determination by the High Court) and this only adds to the rather rough and ready appearance of the proceedings. The phrase "rough and ready" also describes the facilities (toilets, interview rooms, etc) in many of the older magistrates' courts, some of which are a disgrace. Like prisons, many court-buildings are products of a bygone age. Then there is the complaint that many defendants are bewildered by court procedure and are no match for an experienced prosecuting officer. Defendants in magistrates' courts are often unrepresented, even in quite serious cases.

Few would argue that magistrates in general are crudely prejudiced; indeed many courts try quite hard to minimise the handicaps facing accused persons who are unfamiliar with court procedure and rules of evidence. In part the problem stems from our settling for something which is a good deal less than perfect in the interests of speed and economy; but it is also part of a more general problem of achieving "justice" in a subjective as well as an objective sense, to which we return in chapter 8.

The first justification for the speed with which cases are disposed of is that we simply cannot afford a more sophisticated machine to process the vast amount of petty crime (including motoring offences) with which magistrates have to deal. The second (unspoken) justification seems to be that a court which hands out only small sentences can make a few mistakes without anyone suffering very much; and there is a system of appeals to mop up the more obvious errors. (Magistrates cannot impose terms of imprisonment in excess of six months – twelve months for two or more separate offences – and/or fines in excess of £1,000.)

There is much more in the former argument than in the latter. The "smallness" of sentences is a relative concept. A small fine can bear heavily on a person of limited means; those who are least able to present their side of the case in court tend to be poorer people who stand to lose most from the infliction of a fine. The real injustice may in fact lie in imposing on the wealthy offender fines that are *too small*; fining a Jaguar owner £5 for speeding is unfair to the owner of a humbler vehicle who is fined the same amount. A small penalty can have heavy side effects; a third endorsement for a relatively minor motoring offence automatically means the temporary loss of one's driving licence, and this is more than an inconvenience to one who earns his living as a lorry driver or as a travelling salesman. It is all very well to talk about appeals, but access to the appellate system is confined in practice to those who have legal representation – that is, to those who know how to get legal aid or can afford to pay for a lawyer. Very few appeals are successful anyway.

County court and small claims

County courts were first established in 1846 to deal speedily and cheaply with relatively minor civil litigation; their jurisdiction in most matters is limited to a monetary value of £2,000 (but see p. 52) and they are widely used to enforce trading debts. They recently acquired the power to hear undefended divorce petitions. Approximately 1·7 million actions are started in county courts each year, about 60 per cent for sums under £100, and all but a tiny fraction are settled or withdrawn before trial; only 37,000 or so (not counting divorce cases) are actually tried by a circuit judge, and about another 88,000 by court registrars (legally qualified court officials who are empowered to try minor claims). The figures exclude small claims arbitrations (see below).

County courts are cheaper and quicker than the High Court, but they are still fully-fledged courts with formal rules of procedure. This means that, unless a litigant is particularly able and articulate, it is advisable to get a lawyer; this is no problem for a rich man or for a company, but for poorer people it can mean crippling expense or getting legal aid, perhaps both if a legal aid contribution has to be made (see chapter 9). In lawyers' terms a dispute involving (say) £50 may not seem very much, but to many people a sum much less than this would be worth fighting hard for. Yet as soon as litigation is embarked on the lawyers' bill mounts up until it vastly exceeds the amount in dispute. The Law Society told the Consumer Council even as long ago as 1970 that for a one-day hearing in a county court, with expert witnesses on both sides, the cost of recovering £100 would be of the order of £250. Ten years later it is much higher.

In 1970 the Consumer Council published a pamphlet, *Justice Out of Reach: a case for small claims courts*, which recommended giving county court registrars jurisdiction to deal with claims in contract or tort up to £100, and positively forbidding legal representation (an aspect of the proposal which did not endear it to the lawyers). The Nuffield Foundation subsequently sponsored experimental small claims arbitration schemes in Manchester and London. The Administration of Justice Act 1973 permitted county court registrars to order informal arbitration on claims under £75 where both parties agree, and for arbitration to be used in respect of bigger sums where this is ordered by the judge. The limit has been raised to £200 and about 1,200 cases a year are determined by arbitration; use of the procedure is at the discretion of the court, and its impact has, on the whole, been slight.

The National Industrial Relations Court

No book on the relationship between law and politics can afford to ignore the lessons to be learned from the failure of the National Industrial Relations Court, established by the Industrial Relations Act 1971 and abolished by the Labour Government in 1974.

The Court enjoyed the same status as the High Court, but conducted its business informally, attempting to work through conciliation rather than by strict application of legal rules and procedures. Although most of the cases that came before it were uncontroversial its very existence was seen by opponents of the 1971 Act as a provocative attempt to involve the judiciary in party politics. Bitterness reached a peak with a number of cases heard between March and July 1972. In one of these cases three London dockers were committed to prison by the Court for contempt of court by breaching an order forbidding them to picket a container depot employing unregistered labour; major industrial conflict was avoided when the Court of Appeal, employing rather tortuous argument, prudently decided that there was insufficient evidence of contempt. Another group of dockers were imprisoned shortly afterwards in connection with a different dispute about containers, but they were quickly released.

Further bitter controversy arose in the latter part of 1973 over a union recognition dispute at the firm of Con-Mech Ltd. The Amalgamated Union of Engineering Workers, which had held out longer than any other union in its refusal to recognise the NIRC, disobeyed an order of the Court, and the latter ordered that a fine of £75,000 should be levied on it for contempt. Sequestrators[3] acting on the Court's behalf seized money from the union's "political fund" (money earmarked for the sponsoring of parliamentary candidates, etc); this prompted vehement criticisms from left-wing Labour MPs, who reacted even more strongly when Sir John Donaldson, speaking extrajudicially, publicly defended the Court's action. Moves were made in Parliament to have Sir John removed from office; Lord Hailsham, the Lord Chancellor, made things even worse by condemning the actions of the MPs concerned as unconstitutional and thereby added an issue of parliamentary privilege to the mounting crisis.

The NIRC is a fascinating case study of the fine division that can exist between law and politics. No one could deny that the Court played a political role; *any* court called upon to apply politically contentious legislation is open to accusations of partisanship, simply because it cannot please everyone. Its abolition in the summer of 1974 was not surprising.

Lawyers

The content of legal rules and the way in which they are applied are products of the attitudes and values of legislators and judges. Some would argue that the existence of a governing "Establishment" in Britain isolates large sections of the population from the legal and political processes and that laws bear unequally on different classes of people (see chapter 8). At any event, it is clear that those who would understand the law must first understand the lawyers, and the tions that follow will consider some of the characteristics both of the legal profession and of those laymen (magistrates and jurors) who play a major part in the machinery of justice.

A divided profession

There are two main kinds of professional lawyer. In ninety-nine cases out of a hundred where someone has a legal problem (for example, if he wants to make his will, to buy a house, to obtain redress from a debtor, to get compensation for an accident at work, or to resolve a matrimonial matter) he will go to a solicitor – always assuming that he consults a lawyer at all (see chapter 8). If the problem is unusually complicated or if, as only happens in a small proportion of cases, it needs to be dealt with in one of the higher courts (above the level of magistrates' court or county court) then counsel (a barrister) will be called in as well; it is necessary to say "as well" rather than "instead" because there is a firm rule that a barrister can act for a client only if he is first instructed by a solicitor.

The picture is further complicated by the existence of two kinds of barrister – junior barristers and Queen's Counsel (QCs), the latter being called "silks" because of their privilege of wearing silk gowns. There is about one silk for every ten junior barristers and they are chosen by the Lord Chancellor for their ability and distinction; they specialise very largely in advocacy in important cases, and are a reservoir of talent from which most judicial appointments are made. An expensive rule that a silk could not appear in court without a junior was formally abolished in 1976, though the old practice survives.

All this means that a client with a serious legal problem can end up paying three lawyers. First, the solicitor who does the preliminary sifting of the case, and then a silk and junior counsel; if he loses the case he will have to pay for three lawyers on his side and for corresponding representation on the opponent's side. Moreover, if and when the case comes to court the litigant may observe his solicitor, who knows at least as much about the case as counsel, sitting passively at the back, taking virtually no part in the proceedings. Distinguished Queen's Counsel, paid handsomely for his eminence, may sit for half the time apparently doing nothing because the other side is addressing the court. Junior counsel, paid less than the QC who is "leading" him but still paid a lot, may appear to do nothing from beginning to end, unless he is asked to take over the argument of some subsidiary matter or to take over altogether if his leader is called elsewhere.

Added to this, it sometimes happens that barristers find themselves briefed to appear in two places at once. A client may arrive at court expecting to see the cool, confident figure of X who has interviewed him and seen and read all the papers, only to find a flustered Y whose chambers have handed him the brief only that morning. This may not be the barrister's fault (a lot of the trouble is caused by the short notice given of when trials are going to be heard); but one can well understand the feelings of someone who loses his case and then has to pay a large lawyers' bill in circumstances such as these.

The explanation for the division of the legal profession into solicitors and barristers is historical. The alleged justification for the continuing division is that the Bar both specialises in the esoteric art of advocacy and constitutes an exclusive reservoir of talent, in daily contact with the courts, from which future judges can be chosen. Members of the Bar, with their lives revolving around the four Inns of Court in London, have always constituted a closed group in which everyone tends to know everyone else. This grapevine facilitates good communications and mutual trust, but at the high cost of presenting an appearance of remoteness and introverted professional self-interest.

The solicitors' branch of the profession has evolved from the body of men who once did relatively menial clerical tasks ancillary to the work of barristers and the courts; the name probably derives from the old Chancery solicitors who had to "solicit" (cajole, or perhaps bribe) officials of those notoriously dilatory courts to get cases moving. In its modern form the profession dates back to the establishment of the Law Society in 1831 to coordinate the professional lives of those calling themselves solicitors. Now virtually all solicitors belong to the Law Society, which has extensive statutory powers relating to the organisation of the profession and the maintenance of standards of professional conduct; a senior judge, the Master of the Rolls (the "Rolls" being the Roll of Solicitors), has nominal responsibility for adjudging the suitability of solicitors to be officers of the courts, but he delegates his power to the Law Society.

On the barristers' side there is no equivalent to the Law Society. The Inns of Court have much (some would say too much) autonomy, but a number of coordinating bodies exist, the most important being the General Council of the Bar which is elected by the profession.

Professional monopolies

Both branches of the legal profession exercise certain monopolies in aspects of legal work, though some of these are more important and more exclusive than others. It must be stressed, moreover, that the word "monopoly" or the phrase "restrictive practices" are merely descriptive of a particular state of affairs and not necessarily pejorative expressions. One may well argue that the solicitors' monopoly in house conveyancing is contrary to the public interest, but one's case has to be founded on much firmer ground than the assumption that *because* a thing is monopolistic *it follows* that it must be bad.

Barristers have the exclusive right to be appointed judges of the superior courts and the sole right of advocacy in those courts. This is not to say that practising barristers do nothing else but advocacy; junior counsel, in particular, do a lot of preparatory paperwork before a case goes to court, while both QCs and junior barristers are called on to draft opinions on tricky points of law referred to them by solicitors.

Solicitors, or at least some of them, engage in advocacy. They have an unfettered right to argue cases in county courts and in magistrates' courts; they can be given special permission to appear in crown courts (this rarely happens, but permission has been given in a few sparsely populated areas where barristers are thin on the ground); and they are allowed to appear in crown courts in cases where they have represented their client before magistrates and the latter have committed the convicted person to the crown court for sentence, and in appeals to crown courts from magistrates' courts.

Solicitors have an important monopoly which is enshrined in statute law. In conveyancing (the transfer of land and/or buildings from one person to another) only solicitors can act on behalf of the purchaser. Until recently strict scales of fees were fixed by statutory order.

This monopoly has been maintained through fears of fraud, and solicitors argue that property transactions are so important that there must be no room for error through the intervention of bungling amateurs. It is not much use a young couple getting an "amateur" conveyance, only to discover that their nice new house is subject to a demolition order or that the local farmer has a right of way to take his cattle across their back garden. The risk of such occurrences is greatly diminishing with the continuing growth in the system of land registration; and greater flexibility in the cost of conveyancing has come about through the abolition of fixed scales of charges.

Solicitors argue that high fees for conveyancing enable them to subsidise work in other areas (such as litigation in county courts) where they are less than well paid. And some solicitors act without charge or for a nominal fee for poor clients who, for some reason, cannot get legal aid. There is certainly truth in the "subsidy" argument, though the people doing the subsidising (couples buying their homes) are often not particularly well off themselves.

Meanwhile, several self-help groups, notably the National House Owners' Society, have moved into the conveyancing field, exploiting loopholes in the law to challenge the solicitors' monopoly. Such groups have been successfully prosecuted on more than one occasion; but they have certainly helped to bring this controversial issue

out of the obscurity in which many lawyers would no doubt prefer
it to remain (see Appendix 2, para. 10).

The case for fusing the two branches of the profession

Barristers and solicitors live together for the most part in harmony
and mutual respect, but beneath the surface there are deep-rooted
conflicts. Barristers are heavily outnumbered by solicitors; there are
about 4,000 practising barristers in England and Wales as against
32,000 practising solicitors. Thus, on the big question of whether the
two branches should be fused into one it is barristers who tend to feel
most threatened.

On the other hand, solicitors have never quite lived down being the
"junior" side of the profession. Solicitors have much more daily
contact with the public, whereas barristers live in a rather cloistered
world, reinforcing each other's resistance to interference by outsiders. Solicitors sometimes complain about barristers who do not
master their briefs in time and about cases where the barrister's
clerk "double books" him in two courts at once, so that an ill-
prepared last-minute substitute has to be found. For their part,
barristers sometimes complain that solicitors are inordinately slow
in paying their fees.

More criticism comes from outside the professions and one can
discern two main strands of argument. One is that it is quite wrong
for solicitors to be excluded from judicial appointments and from
advocacy in the superior courts; the other is that the two branches
should be fused into one. The two arguments are quite different,
though sometimes (for example, during the Courts Bill debate about
whether solicitors should be eligible for circuit judgeships) it is
hinted that allowing solicitors on to the Bench, or letting them
practise their advocacy in higher courts, would open the floodgates
to fusion. We will concentrate our attention on the question whether
the two branches of the profession should be fused into one. Divided
legal professions (see above) are found on the Continent (and judges
there are appointed quite separately from advocates) but not in the
United States nor even in much of the Commonwealth. The case for
fusion has been put most forcibly in recent years by Michael Zander
and Lord Goodman, both solicitors by training; the case against has
come from successive chairmen of the Bar Council and from succes-

sive Lord Chancellors, including Lord Hailsham and his Labour predecessor, Lord Gardiner. Some writers like R.M. Jackson (also a solicitor) take a middle road, admitting that the profession has a case to answer but doubting whether that case is proven.

The reasons for the divided profession are at least as old as the sixteenth century when barristers threw the attorneys (forerunners of solicitors) out of the Inns of Court. Historical conditions have of course changed since then, but this by itself is an insufficient argument for reform. The question that must be answered is whether, given that the principal features of the legal system we have today are unlikely to change, and making certain value judgments (for example, that giving litigants a fair deal should take priority over giving lawyers a juicy living), would the fusion of the professions be socially advantageous?

The main justification for fusion is economy; it appears ridiculous to pay two (sometimes three or more) expert lawyers to conduct a case, just because it is one in which solicitors cannot appear in court as advocates. Of course, most cases that go to court are dealt with in county courts or magistrates' courts where solicitors can appear; but sometimes solicitors advise clients to brief counsel even in these courts, if only to spread the blame in case something goes wrong. Similarly, a solicitor confronted by a legal problem may play safe by getting counsel's opinion, even if he is reasonably certain that he knows the answer himself.

The real problem arises with more difficult kinds of litigation in the higher courts where there may indeed be need for special skills of advocacy. Even if fusion took place solicitors would have to develop the same degree of expertise as barristers now cultivate; if you took your problem to your local solicitor he might well feel obliged to call in a specialised advocate, just as he does now.

The second argument for fusion is that it might lead to greater efficiency through having cases handled from start to finish by one lawyer. It should be repeated that this is true of most cases at present; few legal problems demand litigation, and when they do, the case can be heard in county courts and magistrates' courts where solicitors can appear anyway. And this brings us back to whether there is a continuing case for specialised advocates. Proponents of the *status quo* point to the United States, where an undivided legal profession has led neither to cheapness nor to speed.

Other arguments used by opponents of fusion are that there is merit in having barristers standing apart from their clients, able to give more dispassionate advice than the family solicitor. Then there is the "cab rank" principle which requires all barristers to take any brief sent to them, so that the most brutal murderer and the political criminal can always find counsel to argue on their behalf. As the famous eighteenth-century advocate Thomas Erskine said, in respect of his defence of Tom Paine on a charge of seditious libel:

From the moment that any advocate can be permitted to say that he will or will not stand between the Crown and the subject arraigned in the Court where he daily sits to practise, from that moment the liberties of England are at an end.

There is much merit in this; in totalitarian countries an enemy of the state is "defended" only as part of a ritual trial process, and (as has already been suggested) the idea of "impartial" hearings is meaningless in such systems in any case in which the state has an interest. But even in Britain the system sometimes breaks down because of the burden of work upon members of the Bar. The defendants in the Angry Brigade trial in 1972 approached fifteen QCs before finding one not engaged elsewhere; assuming that the alibis of counsel in this instance were true, such an occurrence still gives rise to disquieting suspicions in some people's minds. The Bar recognises the very real problem facing solicitors who have to find counsel at short notice, particularly in criminal cases, and there is some talk of improving communications between solicitors and barristers chambers by setting up a centralised "dial-a-barrister" system.

The issue of fusion is a delicate one and is likely to come about (if at all) only in very gradual stages. There are three main trends:

1. slight easing of the right of solicitors to become judges and to practise as advocates;
2. easier transfer of personnel between the two professions;
3. a more common basis for legal education; there would be a lot of sense in having a completely common theoretical training for all lawyers, with a variation in practical work according to whether the lawyer wanted to remain a general practitioner or become a specialist advocate and legal consultant (see Appendix 2, para. 8).

The judges

English judges are, by custom, anonymous figures, detached from the hurly burly of life. It is significant that Anthony Sampson in *The New Anatomy of Britain* thought it a fact worthy of mention that Lord Wilberforce had been seen reading *Sporting Life* in a café in Chancery Lane. There is a welcome tendency for judges to be slightly less remote than in the past, but they, like civil servants, are expected to keep out of the public eye. It is sometimes suggested that the wigs and gowns they wear are intended to underline their anonymity, though Lord Goodman, writing in *The Sunday Times* in 1966, irreverently ventured to doubt "whether the costume of the Ku-Klux-Klan would achieve this objective".

The problem of "political" appointments to the higher judiciary was discussed in chapter 1. This factor is much less a cause for concern than is the inbuilt conservatism of all lawyers; as Professor John Griffith once said, "a man who has had a legal training is never quite the same again". And a senior barrister, later a High Court Judge, put it like this:

> The Lawyer, almost irrespective of his politics, is by training and self-interest a conservative in the affairs of his own profession. The *status quo* is part of his mental capital. Every legal reform robs him of an asset he has worked hard to acquire.[4]

Even the undoubted narrowness of judges' social and educational backgrounds (a vast majority of them come from the top public schools and from Oxbridge) is of less importance than the legalistic values all lawyers inherit through training and professional experience.

Criticism of judges tends to focus upon those at the top of the professional ladder, but table 4.2 shows that there are many more judges at a lower level. And these judges dispose of far more cases than do those of High Court rank and above. Lay magistrates are far and away the most numerous category of judge, and are discussed separately below.

Judicial independence

The constitutional position of judges varies according to their position in the hierarchy. All those above the level of High Court judge are nominally appointed by the monarch on the advice of the

Table 4.2 The Judiciary

Judge	Number serving (1980)	Salary (1980)α	Where they sit
Lord Chancellor	1	£37,000	Occasionally in House of Lords and Privy Council.
Lord Chief Justice	1	£32,792	Presides over Court of Appeal (criminal) and Queen's Bench Divisional Court. Occasionally a trial judge.
Master of the Rolls	1	£30,261	Presides over Court of Appeal (civil).
President of the Family Division	1	£28,961	Presides over Family Division
Lords of Appeal in Ordinary	10	£30,261	House of Lords and Privy Council.
Lords Justices of Appeal*	18	£27,799	Court of Appeal (civil and criminal).
High Court Judges† Queen's Bench Chancery Family	47 12‡ 17	£25,886	Trial judges in their respective divisions and on appeal in the Divisional Courts of those divisions. QB judges sit with Lords Justices on appeals to Court of Appeal (criminal); also try civil and criminal matters in some crown courts.
Circuit judges	295	£18,015	Trials and appeals in crown courts.
Recorders (part time)	377	£95 a day	Crown courts.
Stipendiary magistrates London Provincial cities	40 11	§	Sit as magistrates in some London courts and in certain other large cities.
Lay magistrates	34,000 (about 9,000 of whom do not sit)	Expenses only	Sit as magistrates and juvenile justices in courts throughout Britain. Sit with judge in crown courts on appeal from other magistrates.

α In July 1980 further salary increases were announced, ranging from 8·1 per cent for the Lord Chief Justice to 12·8 per cent for circuit judges. Since 1971 the salaries of the higher judiciary have been kept under review by the Top Salaries Review Body.

* Abbreviated to LJ (plural, LJJ): thus "Smith and Brown, LJJ" means "Lords Justices Smith and Brown".

† Also called *puisne* (pronounced "puny") judges. Abbreviated to J and JJ (see above note).

‡ Including a Vice Chancellor who is head of the Division.

§ The Chief Metropolitan Stipendiary Magistrate gets £18,015; other Metropolitan Stipendiaries get £16.202.

Note. This list excludes Scottish and Northern Irish judges, as well as officials like Masters of the Supreme Court, and county court registrars, who perform certain ancillary judicial functions; it also excludes such "specialised" judges as the President of the Lands Tribunal.

Prime Minister, and the latter usually takes his cue from the Lord Chancellor. The Lord Chancellor appoints judges at and below the rank of High Court judge.

Written into legislation dating back to the Act of Settlement 1701 is the principle that senior judges hold office "during good behaviour" and in the event of misconduct can be removed only on an address to the Queen by both Houses of Parliament.[5] Their salaries are a standing charge on the Consolidated Fund and cannot be altered through the annual Estimates. These much-vaunted devices for securing the freedom of judges from political pressures are illusory; we have no written constitution, and legislation could be passed at any time altering the position of the judiciary, though obviously there might be *political* difficulties in doing this.

Parliament is not generally allowed to criticise particular judges except on a motion for removal. According to Henry Cecil, between 1700 and 1963 the conduct of seventeen High Court judges has been complained of in Parliament; only one, the Irish judge Sir Jonah Barrington, was removed, in 1830.[6] In 1973 187 Labour MPs put down a motion for the removal of the President of the National Industrial Relations Court, Sir John Donaldson. In January 1978 there was a motion to remove an Old Bailey judge for allegedly racist remarks he made when summing up in a race relations trial.

The dismissal of any rank of judge is clearly not something to be contemplated lightly, though the removal of lower-tier judges is in theory a matter purely for the Lord Chancellor's discretion. One problem has always been the case of judges who become prematurely senile or infirm; the Administration of Justice Act 1973 empowers the

Lord Chancellor, after consultation with senior judges, to declare vacant the office of any judge of High Court rank and above who is no longer capable of discharging his duties and who is incapable of taking the decision to resign. The Lord Chancellor has long had such a power in respect of the lower judiciary.

The salaries and pensions of judges have recently been revised. County court judges (now circuit judges) have long been required to retire at seventy-two; now newly appointed High Court and appellate judges must retire at seventy-five. In the nature of things, judges tend to be appointed at a fairly advanced age, so until the new retiring ages begin to bite the Bench will be top-heavy with elderly men, particularly in the appellate courts.

Salaries, as can be seen in table 4.2, are considerable, but less than can be earned in the top ranks of the Bar and lower too than higher managerial and professional salaries in industry and commerce. But judges are expected to regard the dignity of office as ample recompense; there was considerable criticism of the former High Court judge Sir Henry Fisher who, in 1971, left the Bench after only two years to join a City banking firm.

Public criticism of the judiciary is today (as with criticism of the monarch) much rarer than was the case in the last century. Nineteenth-century legal journals did not mince their words when they disapproved of a judicial appointment. Of the appointment of Mr Justice Ridley by Lord Halsbury in 1897 the *Law Journal* wrote: "the appointment can be defended on no ground whatsoever. It would be easy to name fifty members of the Bar with a better claim."

That such observations would be unthinkable today reflects the movement away from political criteria in judicial appointments towards the selection only of those with the right professional qualities. It reflects too an overdeveloped deference on the part of commentators to the isolationism of the judiciary, though in recent years judges have been rather more willing to show their public *personae*. It should be noted also that judges, like civil servants, are discouraged from bandying words with critics in public. An instance of a more open treatment of the subject in the media (though hardly very typical) was the publication in *The Sunday Times* of a long article about the Master of the Rolls, Lord Denning. Based on an interview with the judge, the article delved deeply and critically into Lord Denning's individualistic approach to legal problems.[7] Lord Denning himself has since gone into print (see Bibliography).

The Justice subcommittee's report on judges

In 1972 a subcommittee of the organisation Justice published *The Judiciary*, a report containing wideranging proposals for reform. Its main conclusions were that:

1. the Lord Chancellor should be obliged to consult a special advisory committee when making judicial appointments;
2. the social backgrounds of judges are too narrow (though this is not simply to be remedied by appointing more "working class" judges);
3. there should be a broadly based training scheme for new judges, and study leave for those already serving; a judicial staff college should be set up;
4. the judicial process should be accompanied by less ritual;
5. judges should have the assistance of "law clerks" to do research for them (though it is doubtful whether they would want them);
6. judges should be encouraged to lead more "normal" social lives;
7. there should be independent machinery for investigating complaints against judges;
8. it should be possible to remove judges for incapacity (this is now possible under the Administration of Justice Act 1973 – see above); judges should be required to have regular medical examinations;
9. solicitors should be eligible to become judges; and academic lawyers should be eligible for appointment to the appellate courts.

In 1979 a very modest scheme of judicial training was instituted following the report of a working party under Lord Justice Bridges. In 1936 Lord Chief Justice Hewart told the assembled throng at the Lord Mayor's Banquet that, ''Her Majesty's Judges are satisfied with the almost universal admiration in which they are held''. The quality of the judiciary is generally high, with most of the exceptions at the lower levels, but this does not entitle either the lawyer or the citizen to be as complacent as Lord Hewart.

Magistrates

Criticism of magistrates' courts reached a peak between the two world wars largely because, as R.M. Jackson[8] points out, middle-class motoring offenders came into contact with these courts for the first time ''and they did not like what they found''. A Royal Commission reported on the subject in 1948[9] and, while it accepted the need for lay magistrates, it made important recommendations, many of which were enacted in the Justices of the Peace Act 1949.

The system of lay magistrates has been criticised because of the overtly party-political nature of many appointments to the Bench. When the Royal Commission reported it was common for the local advisory committees (first set up in 1910 to advise the Lord Chancellor in appointing magistrates) to operate a "spoils" system, carving up appointments between the stalwarts of local political party organisations. The Royal Commission rightly recognised that it is unrealistic to expect magistrates to be political eunuchs, and that in practice the kind of person who is likely to want to be a magistrate is also likely to be politically active in the community.

In recent years advisory committees have been told to keep a better balance in their recommendations; Lord Gardiner, in particular, campaigned to get more working-class people and more women on to the Bench. To these ends advisory committees (which used to keep themselves anonymous, particularly in rural districts, to avoid being pestered by aspirants to office) have tended to operate more publicly; some even advertise vacancies on the Bench.

Some important reforms have taken place recently. Magistrates must undergo training; sentencing conferences are organised by the Lord Chief Justice; and there is now a compulsory retiring age of seventy. It is now no longer possible for local mayors to sit as magistrates by virtue of their office.

One of the most ambiguously defined positions in the legal system is that of the magistrates' clerk; the latter administers the magistrates' courts and advises the justices on points of law. Since 1949 justices' clerks have had to be barristers or solicitors of five years standing; however, the clerks who sit in most magistrates' courts are much less highly qualified "court clerks", deputising for the clerk to the justices. They are there to guide the court on matters of law and procedure, but there is a difficult dividing line between giving guidance and usurping, or appearing to usurp, powers that should only be exercised by the magistrate. When the justices retire to consider verdict and/or sentence, the clerk can be asked to retire with them to advise on problems of law or to explain what sentences have been imposed in similar cases in the past. Even if he sticks firmly to his proper role it may *appear* to those in court as if the clerk has played an undue part in deciding the outcome.

Why do we not have a system in which lay magistrates have a

subordinate role (as assessors) and employ legally qualified chairmen? In that event, as when a clerk sits in court with a stipendiary magistrate, the clerk would become pre-eminently a court administrator and the difference between his role and that of the Bench would be clearcut. Such a proposal is not practical politics (*a*) because the system of lay justice, for all its faults, has several virtues; (*b*) because legally qualified chairmen would cost a lot of public money; and (*c*) because the lay magistracy is a formidable pressure group with which politicians are loath to tangle[10].

Juries

In feudal England juries were used to assist the courts by their special knowledge of local circumstances and of the parties to the case. Today, however, the whole emphasis has changed; personal knowledge of an accused person would debar someone from serving on a jury, though the sort of extensive inquiry into the antecedents of potential jurors, which is so prominent a feature of criminal trials in the United States, is unknown in the English trial process. Juries, usually consisting of twelve members, are used in all criminal trials on indictment; since 1967, majority verdicts (i.e. permitting one or two jurors to dissent) have been allowed in criminal trials. Juries have become much rarer in civil proceedings, though they are still sometimes used in defamation cases.

Juries are arbiters of fact, and take their guidance on points of law from the judge. Some commentators (including Lord Devlin) regard the jury system as a means of reflecting public morality in the criminal law; this view seems unrealistic. Juries are at their worst in dealing with complex matters like fraud and in the assessment of damages in civil actions. In recent years the courts have strongly discouraged the use of juries in personal injury cases.

The jury system was examined by the Morris Committee, which reported in 1965.[11] Many people have seen the main problem as being the socially unrepresentative character of juries; they have often been described as "middle-class, middle-aged and middle-minded". At the time of the Morris inquiry only ratepayers aged between twenty-one and sixty could serve as jurors; the Criminal Justice Act 1972 extended eligibility to all registered electors between eighteen and sixty-five. But it is still ·open to question whether juries, however they are constituted, are the bastions of liberty that some would have us believe, though no doubt they can sometimes soften the harsh application of the law in ways not open to judges who are obliged to give reasoned decisions (see later section on acquittals).

Juries are regarded, rightly or wrongly, as an important part of the machinery of justice, but we know little about them. Occasionally, hair-raising stories leak out about dissentient members being bullied into agreeing so that everyone can go home in time for tea (the appeal courts will hardly ever interfere with the jury's verdict, even where serious irregularities are alleged). Social scientists, notably at the University of Chicago, have researched into simulated jury decisions and have obtained interesting results; but ultimately one cannot be sure that synthetic decisions based on simulated data are equivalent to the real thing.[12]

In 1979 the *New Statesman* published details of what had taken place in the jury room in the Thorpe conspiracy trial. The Lord Chief Justice later expressed concern about such leaks but held that there had been no contempt of court. Another vexed issue has been "jury vetting". The Juries Act 1974 says that only those with serious criminal convictions may be excluded from juries. In 1975 the then Attorney General issued guidelines specifying "exceptional types of case of public importance" (including ones involving strong political motives, eg. IRA terrorism) where potential jurors' police and special branch records may be inspected by the prosecution, with the consent of the Director of Public Prosecutions. The practice was exposed in an official secrets trial in 1978; and it aroused grave concern in the trial of six self-confessed anarchists in September 1979 when leaks revealed that the criteria adopted by the vetters were disquietingly wide (eg. they noted the fact that someone was a squatter, and that another had complained against the police). You cannot have semi-random 'juries any more than you can have semi-fresh eggs. There are suspicions that quite a lot of covert vetting, outside the 1975 guidelines, may be going on. Is there really much difference between *vetting* a jury to ensure that IRA bombers are not tried by fellow members of the IRA and *rigging* a jury to exclude those who, because they have complained against the police, may be unsympathetic to the prosecution? On the other hand, in the USA, extensive and time-consuming pre-trial vetting by both prosecution and defence is seen as an essential pre-requisite of a fair trial. So perhaps it is the method rather than the principle which we should really be worrying about? The 1975 guidelines were amended in July 1980 to provide (marginally) better safeguards.[13]

5 Administrative Law

It is quite as necessary to provide against being ruled by judges as it is to guard against being judged by ministers.

R.M. JACKSON

The scope of administrative law is much easier to describe than to define. The truth probably lies between two extreme attitudes to politics and law, neither of which necessarily corresponds to the reality of any existing political system. At one extreme one might imagine a state ruled by an absolute despot who has the legal system completely under his thumb, the ruler himself being completely above the law and immune from its sanctions. At the other extreme it is possible to conceive of a state where the rulers were under the control of lawyers, with every act of government being assessed against some legal standard (perhaps laid down in a legal code or a written constitution) interpreted by the courts. In such a state the exercise of political and administrative discretion would give way to a strict adherence to rules and precedents.

Both these situations are caricatures. The first, a state ruled without any reference to the law, may lead one to think of autocracies like Hitler's Germany where the government exercised close control over the working of the courts and made sure that the judges were politically "reliable". Our democratic instincts bristle indignantly at the idea of government ruling by decree; there should, one feels, be at least *some* externally defined standards maintained by independent, or at least relatively independent, bodies like the courts.

The contrary case of a state where politics is subsumed under law may lead us to consider countries like the United States with extensive written constitutions which are enforceable by the courts. As two distinguished commentators have written of the United States:

Constitutional issues permeate American law and life to an extent
that foreign observers find incredible. Americans have become a
people of constitutionalists, who substitute litigation for legislation and see constitutional questions lurking in every case.
American society, more than any other, is imbued with legal
ideas and dominated by lawyers and lawyer-judges.[1]

But this is a long way from saying that the United States is actually
ruled by judges and lawyers; indeed the "checks and balances"
written into the Constitution are designed expressly to avoid the overconcentration of power in any one part of the machinery of government.

Rule by the courts might appear, at first sight, to be infinitely
preferable to arbitrary and lawless despotism, but is this necessarily
so? In countries like ours government is based on the principle that
the job of governing should be left to representatives who, on balance,
can be trusted to act effectively and fairly. In practice we may find
plenty of grounds for complaining that governments are "unrepresentative" or "inefficient" and that the real decisions are taken by
non-elected civil servants anyway, but this is another matter. The
point is that, in the last analysis, it is *governments* who must govern
and it is not up to the courts to do their job for them.

There is, moreoever, a basic difference between the respective
techniques of politicians and judges. An English judge decides legal
disputes by applying general principles of law (derived from precedents and statutes) to particular facts. Such a legalistic approach is
inappropriate to a policy decision about whether to build a new
motorway or whether to cut government expenditure by abolishing
free school milk. The policy-maker cannot follow rigid rules of
precedent, except to the very limited extent of learning by his previous
successes and failures.

Inseparably bound up with policy decisions are administrative
issues of how policy is applied to particular cases; and administration usually embodies some legal constraints. For example, if the
Secretary of State for the Environment needs to acquire land to build
a road (after reaching a policy decision that a new road is necessary)
he must, by law, follow procedures laid down in Acts of Parliament.
The proposals must be publicised and the minister is obliged to hold

a public inquiry into objections; such inquiries differ markedly, as we shall see, from courts of law but they, like the minister himself, are required to observe certain standards of procedural fairness; if the minister or his inquiry inspector depart from the legal requirements imposed on them by statute and by common law (such as the rules of "natural justice") an aggrieved party can seek a remedy in the courts.

Consider also the example of free school milk. The Heath government's decision to abolish free milk was, by definition, absolutely legal since there is in Britain no higher authority such as a written constitution to refute the legality of Acts of Parliament. The Education (School Milk) Act 1971, once passed, was binding upon the courts. Equally, if a government decides to repeal any such Act this decision will also be binding once the requisite legislation has been duly enacted.

In the case of the school milk legislation the courts were called on to adjudicate, not on the constitutional propriety of a controversial piece of legislation but on the conduct of local councillors who defied the Act. Councillors who insisted on providing free milk were held to have infringed the legal doctrine of *ultra vires* (see below) and to have been properly surcharged by the district auditor, whose task it is to see that authorities spend money only where expressly authorised to do so by Act of Parliament.

It should now be clear that administrative law has nothing to do with courts *controlling* governments by substituting their own decisions for those of politicians and administrators. But it does have to do with the legal rules which impose constraints upon what governments can legally do, always remembering that governments can change those rules almost whenever they like. The extent of these constraints varies widely according to the nature of the political system, on political circumstances at a given time (for example, the courts are much less willing to curb the executive in times of war or national emergency), and on the courage of judges in standing up to the government. The basic problem of administrative law is *how far* the administrative process should be regulated by law.

There is an analogy with the role of the referee in a game of football. Some games are ruined by a referee who blows his whistle for every trivial infringement of the rules; others degenerate into a brawl because the referee is too timid. The ideal lies between the two extremes. A good system of administrative law will provide a framework of standards for good administrative practice, without attempting to substitute legalistic values and techniques for political ones. There is a perennial problem of achieving a satisfactory balance.

Administrative justice
The phrase "administrative justice" is sometimes used interchangeably with "administrative law"; but to confuse law with justice in this context obscures a fundamental problem.

Those who govern a complex society tend to be left with a good deal of scope for discretion and personal judgment. It is clearly nonsense to suppose that every voter approves of, or even knows about, everything the government does, even though that government may claim a mandate from the ballot box for its actions. Since the days of Edmund Burke it has been a well-established principle that MPs are representatives rather than mandated delegates; even crucially important issues are not put to a referendum (the EEC case and that of devolution being notable exceptions).

In practice the job of governing has to do with setting goals in terms of "the public good" and directing policy-making and administration towards those goals. But there are three basic problems:

1. Not everyone will agree about what constitutes the public good or about the means of achieving it.
2. Whether or not there is broad agreement about the public good, individual citizens may be adversely affected by decisions made in the wider public interest.
3. Those responsible for making political and administrative decisions are human, and therefore fallible. They may neglect to observe rules based on law or on commonsense standards of fairness or courtesy; they may be corrupt, inept or inefficient.

The first problem is the stuff of which politics is made, and the law hardly plays any part in it. The second problem sums up the difference between administrative *law* and administrative *justice*. Once a government has decided, in what it considers to be the public interest, to build new motorways, to clear slums or to introduce non-selective secondary education, it has to contend with individuals whose lives are disturbed in consequence. A person whose house is compulsorily purchased or whose child is denied the education his parents consider most appropriate may have little sympathy for talk of the "public interest"; but provided there is no illegality in the decision administrative law cannot help them. The only remedy against policy decisions one does not like is political pressure: lobbying MPs, ministers and councillors, press campaigns and petitions, and, if all else fails, lying down in front of the bulldozer when the demolition men arrive.

The remedies available under administrative law relate principally to the third kind of problem, where a public authority acts outside established rules of law and fair practice. There is a wide range of different remedies, jumbled together in a rather untidy way. In some cases the remedy lies in the courts (usually the Divisional Court of the Queen's Bench Division); others may be dealt with by tribunals or inquiries; the idea of an "ombudsman" has become fashionable in recent years. The machinery of administrative justice will be outlined in the sections that follow.

Control of public authorities by the courts: the ultra vires rule
It is important to bear in mind that the courts (for reasons already discussed) refrain from meddling in the merits of policy decisions; "British judges", Schwartz and Wade remind us, "are acutely conscious that they are at the mercy of a sovereign Parliament, which can quickly clip their wings if they fly too high."[2] Moreover, the effectiveness of judicial control varies from era to era; the two decades after the Second World War probably saw the courts at their most timid, but from the mid-1960s onwards there has been a marked increase in the willingness of judges to hold the Executive to account for its actions.

The principal machinery by which the courts exercise their supervision is as follows:

1. the *ultra vires* rule and various derivatives of it.
2. appeals to the courts under the provisions of various Acts.
3. ordinary legal actions in contract, tort, etc, against public authorities.

Ultra vires is a Latin expression meaning "outside the powers". Most public bodies such as local authorities and public corporations have their powers defined by statute and must not do anything which lies outside those powers; even a minister may have some of his functions specified in an Act, the terms of which he must strictly observe. This is not the same as requiring him *only* to perform those functions conferred on him by statute; but if, for example, a minister makes a statutory instrument which goes beyond the terms of the parent Act, then the instrument is said to be *ultra vires*. The doctrine of *ultra vires* as applied to local authorities has been somewhat softened by the provisions of the Local Government Act 1972.

In about 1920 the London Borough of Fulham decided to build a municipal laundry; it maintained that it had statutory power to do this by virtue of nineteenth-century Acts authorising the building of public baths and wash-houses. But, even though the authority was clearly acting in good faith in accordance with its view of the public interest, the courts ruled that the action was *ultra vires*.[3] This is the doctrine of *ultra vires* at its most straightforward, but it goes further. Even if an authority appears to have statutory authority for its actions the courts may examine the motives for those actions. When the Borough of Westminster built the subway linking the underground station with the Houses of Parliament, it invoked a statute empowering it to build public conveniences, and public conveniences were in fact incorporated into the subway complex; the courts took a long hard look at whether this was a pretext for building a tunnel, or whether the tunnels merely gave legitimate and necessary access to the lavatories before giving the authority the benefit of the doubt.[4]

Several important manifestations of the *ultra vires* principle have arisen from the rule (now modified)[5] that members of a local authority which incurs unauthorised expenditure can be surcharged (that is, made to pay the unauthorised sum out of their own pockets) by the government-appointed district auditors who check local authority accounts. Councillors could appeal either to the courts or to the Secretary of State for the Environment (depending on the amount of the surcharge) against auditors' decisions. In *Roberts* v *Hopwood*[6] the courts upheld an auditor's surcharge imposed on members of Poplar Council (then Labour controlled) for subsidising the wages of its employees at the ratepayers' expense, at a time when wages generally were falling, even though the Act said that the authority could pay such wages as it thought fit; in the House of Lords the authority's decision was denounced as displaying "eccentric principles of socialist philanthropy". More recently, the councillors of Clay Cross in Derbyshire were surcharged nearly £7,000 for (in effect) subsidising rents in defiance of the controversial Housing Finance Act 1972.

Even a minister, exercising wide discretionary powers derived from an Act of Parliament, may find the courts requiring him to exercise those powers "reasonably". *Padfield* v *Minister of Agriculture*[7] was a case arising out of a statutory milk marketing scheme. The Act provides that if milk producers complain about the working of the scheme the Minister can, "if he so directs", refer the complaint to a special committee. In this instance the Minister refused to do so; when the producers took the case to court, the Minister argued that he had complete discretion in the matter, but the House of Lords held that he was exercising his discretion unreasonably. The producers' victory was a hollow one because when the complaints committee reported back to the Minister recommending that the complaint be upheld, the Minister rejected the recommendation. *Padfield* ranks with the *Tameside* case in 1976 (see below) as showing the power of the courts to require ministers to keep strictly within the law.

Natural justice

An important extension of the *ultra vires* principle (though some writers treat it separately) is to be seen in the rules of "natural justice". These have evolved over the years as a means whereby the superior courts could impose minimum standards of fairness upon inferior bodies acting judicially or "quasi judicially", and are very important in fields where some issue is in dispute and some public authority is charged with resolving that dispute. There are two main rules, both commonly described by Latin phrases: *audi alterem partem* (hear the other side) and *nemo judex in causa sua* (no one can be a judge in his own cause).

The most important case in recent years is *Ridge* v *Baldwin*[8] in which a police chief constable appealed to the House of Lords against his dismissal by the local watch committee; he succeeded on the grounds that he had not been given a proper chance to present his side of the case. The rule against bias has always been strictly applied. One case involved the decision of a local planning committee taken in the presence of a member with a financial interest in the outcome of the proceedings; although he took no part in the deliberations it was held that the outward *appearance* of bias was enough to invalidate the decision.

Finally, the courts can intervene when there is "an error of law on the face of the record"; if a public body bases its decisions on a false proposition of law which appears in the public record of the decision then the decision can be quashed (this is one reason why it is considered so important for administrative tribunals to give reasons for their decisions).

Legal proceedings against the Crown

Until the enactment of the Crown Proceedings Act 1947 it was very difficult to bring civil actions against public servants. If you wanted to sue for breach of contract you had to get leave (a "petition of right") from the Attorney-General. An old convention that "the King can do no wrong" meant that there was no direct means of suing a public servant in tort; an absurd pretence was resorted to whereby a named civil servant would be put up as a "dummy defendant" and the damages against him would be paid by his department. This piece of nonsense was swept away by the 1947 Act.

Public authorities and their employees acting in their official capacities can now be sued like anyone else, though there are some special features which do not apply in actions against private individuals. For example, public contracts can differ from private ones in that a contract made by one authority does not necessarily bind its successors; if this were not the case then a change of government (local or central) would mean the newly elected administration finding itself bound by the promises of the opposing party. It should also be noted that public authorities can do many things which could not legally be done by individuals or private organisations (for example, they can decide to knock down people's houses), but, as we have seen, they have to stick strictly to the powers conferred on them and follow fair rules of procedure.

Crown privilege

In 1939 the experimental submarine *Thetis* sank during naval trials with the loss of ninety-nine lives. Relatives of the victims sued the builders of the submarine and called on them to disclose various documents relating to its construction. Although the government was not a party to the proceedings it was understandably concerned lest secret information should fall into enemy hands, and it invoked a device called Crown privilege whereby the courts, on application by a minister, can forbid the disclosure of documents as contrary to the public interest.

On appeal[9] the House of Lords held that in this case the Crown's claim should be upheld, thus ensuring that the plaintiffs lost their action; but in the course of their judgments the Law Lords laid down broad principles which went well beyond the circumstances of the case. In particular, their Lordships held that once a minister has sworn that disclosure is contrary to the public interest the court cannot question this or examine the documents for themselves.

Following the *Thetis* case, it soon became apparent that Crown privilege was being invoked in cases where the risk to the public interest seemed very slight. In one case,[10] for example, a prisoner transferred to a prison hospital was brutally attacked by a fellow prisoner. He sued the prison authorities for negligence in failing to keep proper watch on a prisoner with a propensity to violence; but his action failed because, despite judicial criticism of the Crown's action in invoking privilege, he could not get disclosure of his attacker's case-history.

The *Thetis* doctrine was criticised on many occasions, but the courts could not challenge a ruling of the House of Lords. It was not until 1968 that the House of Lords itself, using its new power to over-rule its previous decisions modified the rule to allow judges to examine the relevant documents to determine whether the minister's claim to privilege looks plausible.[11] Clearly, however, the courts will be very wary of substituting their own view of the public interest for that of the competent minister.

Apart from the importance of Crown privilege as a small but important device whereby the government can interfere with private litigation in order to safeguard the public interest, the manner in which the law was changed illustrates both the gradualism of judicial law-making and the sort of mess that the law can get into if precedents are set too wide.

The Donoughmore and Franks Reports

The early part of the twentieth century saw a rapid expansion in government activity, accompanied by a tendency to transfer the task of resolving disputes in matters like social security and town planning from the courts to newly created bodies like tribunals. Heeding the warnings of Professor Dicey about threats to the "rule of law" in emulating Continental administrative law, many lawyers were very concerned about these new developments.

In a well-known polemic, *The New Despotism*, published in 1929, Lord Chief Justice Hewart denounced a tendency towards "administrative lawlessness":

> The exercise of arbitrary power is neither law nor justice, administrative or at all. The very conception of "law" is a conception of something involving the application of known rules and principles, and a regular course of procedure. There are no rules or principles which can be said to be the rules or principles of this astonishing variety of administrative "law", nor is there any regular course of procedure for its application.

Stung by these criticisms, the government appointed a Committee on Ministers' Powers under the chairmanship of Lord Donoughmore. After deliberating for three years it reported[12] that new-fangled devices like administrative tribunals were here to stay, but that safeguards were necessary. In particular, it said that tribunals should adhere to "natural justice", that reasoned decisions should be given and that inspectors' reports following public inquiries should be published. It rejected emphatically any proposal to set up special administrative courts.

The report thus vindicated the *status quo*; its specific proposals were largely ignored. In the 1950s the state of administrative law became once more an issue for public debate. In 1954 the Minister of Agriculture resigned following disclosures of some double-dealing in the transfer of some farming land at Crichel Down, in which civil servants in his department were held to be at fault.[13] In 1955 a departmental committee was set up under the chairmanship of Sir Oliver (now Lord) Franks to look at the system of statutory tribunals and public planning inquiries. Its terms of reference in fact bore little relevance to the sort of departmental "maladministration" which had occurred in the Crichel Down case.

The Franks proposals[14] were substantially implemented in the Tribunals and Inquiries Act 1958. Great stress was laid on the need for "openness, fairness and impartiality" in tribunal and inquiry proceedings. Following its recommendations, a Council on Tribunals was set up to supervise the operation of tribunals and inquiries and to deal with complaints about them from the public; the procedure for appointing members and chairmen of tribunals was tightened up; much more systematic provision was for appeals to lie to the courts from tribunal decisions; parties appearing before tribunals and inquiries can obtain reasons for decisions on request and (to many people's surprise) the government implemented the recommendation that inquiry inspectors' reports should be made public.

There are two views of the Franks reforms. Many law books think they constitute a considerable improvement. But R.M. Jackson[15] denounces the Franks Committee for giving too much weight to the evidence of lawyers and deplores the importing of formal lawyers' notions of procedural justice into administrative machinery. This difference of opinion reflects the problem already discussed of how far it is appropriate to let lawyers' ideas and procedures impose themselves on administration.

Public inquiries[16]
Someone wishing to build an extension to their house or to convert their home into a fish and chip shop must get planning permission from the local planning authority. If permission is refused, there is a statutory right of appeal to the Department of the Environment; the Minister will send an inspector (who is a civil servant) to conduct a public inquiry. At the end of the inquiry, at which the applicant, the authority and (usually) other interested parties such as neighbours, will have been given a chance to tell their side of the story in a fairly informal setting, the inspector goes away to write his report.

Here there arises a slight ambiguity about the inspector's position. At one time his task was merely to collect evidence and present it, with a recommendation, to the minister, who would then decide the matter (though in 97 per cent of cases his decision was the same as his inspector's). This still happens in a lot of cases, but the Town and Country Planning Act 1968 provided that minor planning disputes can be designated by the minister as appropriate to be decided by the inspector himself. This means that the oft-cited distinction between an inquiry and a tribunal (that the former is a device for advising ministers, while the latter is a device for deciding cases on the spot) is no longer strictly accurate. About 85 per cent of appeals are determined by inspectors.

Public inquiries are applicable to many kinds of administrative decision, particularly (though not exclusively) in town and country planning. Historically they derive from the inquiries held into private

Bills – the method of land acquisition etc, used prior to twentieth-century planning Acts.

We have encountered one situation where the minister (via his inspector) arbitrates in a dispute about planning between a citizen and his local authority. He is also an arbiter in cases where the planning proposal is issued by the local authority itself – for example, where the authority issues a compulsory purchase order. In both these kinds of case the citizen might be excused for supposing that an inquiry is something akin to the "neutral" arbitration carried out in a court or a tribunal. There is, however, a clear difference when the minister holds an inquiry into a scheme initiated by *himself*.

The New Towns Acts empower ministers to designate certain areas to receive population overspill; the legislation provides for the holding of public inquiries into local objections. But as the minister is himself a principal party to the inquiry is this not a flagrant breach of natural justice?

The question arose in a case called *Franklin* v *the Minister of Town and Country Planning*[17] While the New Towns Bill was still before Parliament the minister responsible went to the town of Stevenage and made a rather provocative speech proclaiming his plan to designate the area as a new town in spite of objections. An inquiry was duly held, and the minister finalised the scheme. The objectors challenged the validity of the inquiry on the grounds that the minister had prejudged the issue, rendering the inquiry a farce.

The House of Lords upheld the minister. It pointed out, in effect, that "bias" is built into the system since the minister would hardly initiate a proposal to which he was not committed. The minister's only duty under the Act was to hold an inquiry and give objectors a fair hearing. His functions are administrative rather than judicial.

This view has been upheld in subsequent judicial decisions, and was endorsed by the Franks Committee. However, frustrated objectors at inquiries can hardly be blamed for viewing the proceedings with a measure of cynicism. Lawyers may be clear in their minds that inquiries are not "courts" – but the citizen may not see things in quite the same way. The controversy has revived with motorway inquiries; disruption of which led the Department of Transport in 1978 to give them much wider terms of reference.

Special tribunals[18]

Specialised tribunals are by no means a novelty in the English legal system. There are, for example, tribunals of inquiry set up to investigate matters of urgent public concern; there are disciplinary tribunals attached to professional bodies; there are courts that operate outside the ordinary judicial process like ecclesiastical courts, courts martial and the Court of Chivalry. The tribunals we are about to consider are set up by statute to resolve disputes in various aspects of social administration and fall, for the most part, under the purview of the Council on Tribunals.

The first of these tribunals was set up under the National Insurance Act 1911 to settle disputes arising out of Lloyd George's health and unemployment insurance schemes. Today there are about 2,000 tribunals of about fifty different types. Some, like Rent Tribunals, Industrial Tribunals, National Insurance Tribunals and Income Tax Tribunals sit almost continuously and in many centres. Others, like the Independent Schools Tribunal hardly ever sit at all. Tribunals come and go with shifts in public policy; National Service Exemption Tribunals were clearly no longer needed after the abolition of conscription.

There is considerable variation in the way in which different tribunals work. The Lands Tribunal and the Transport Tribunal have a status on a level with the High Court. Others, like the Rent Tribunal, operate very informally. There is an appeal directly to the courts from the decisions of a few tribunals (though not on the *merits* of decisions); but in other cases the Queen's Bench Divisional Court has the power to quash tribunal decisions for an error of law on the face of the record.

The strengths of the tribunal system may be summed up as follows:

1. They operate more quickly than courts (though this ceases to be true if there is extensive machinery for appeal).
2. They are much cheaper than courts (though some people insist on being professionally represented; there is no legal aid, except in the **Lands Tribunal and the Commons Tribunal – see Appendix 2, para. 6**).
3. They operate in a specialised field and can therefore concentrate on building up expertise in that field; their chairmen are usually legally qualified while the two lay members are selected from panels of suitably qualified people.
4. They are more flexible than courts and do not work through precedent (though naturally they will try to be consistent and must, in

any event, work strictly within a framework of the relevant legal rules).

5. They operate less formally than courts; thus they can relax the strict rules of evidence and dispense with legal mumbo-jumbo.

The main weaknesses of the tribunal system are:

1. A tendency to try to behave too much like courts (see below).
2. There may be the *appearance* of injustice in the fact that tribunals, though "independent", are run by the Department with an interest in the subject matter of the dispute (though, since the 1958 Act, chairmen have been appointed from panels appointed by the Lord Chancellor). The clerks to supplementary benefit appeal tribunals are civil servants from the Department of Health and Social Security, on secondment.
3. There are too many *kinds* of tribunal, with overlapping juris-dictions (as in those dealing separately with rents and with rating).
4. Even though procedures are relatively informal, lay people, particularly those from humble backgrounds who constitute the bulk of those applying for social security etc, are likely to be very much out of their depth (and many potential applicants never go near tribunals because they do not know their rights).

Legal aid as such may not be the answer; representation by pro-fessional people other than lawyers may be appropriate in some tribunals – a pilot "Surveyors' Aid" scheme has been tried in London to assist people appearing before Rent Assessment Com-mittees. And R.M. Jackson suggests that lawyers may defeat the whole object: "a lawyer who sails into a tribunal believing he is bringing the light of the law into outer darkness . . . is simply a menace". In many cases where voluntary groups (such as local tenants' rights groups, or the Child Poverty Action Group) have provided voluntary representation, success rates have increased dramatically; considerable success has been achieved by the National Council for Civil Liberties, helping people who appear before Mental Health Tribunals. Referring to Supplementary Benefits Tribunals, Paul Harrison points out that:

Among appellants who neither attended nor were represented, the success rate was only 6 per cent in the three months to June 1972. Of those who attended without representation, 23 per cent were successful. But 30 per cent of those who attended and were represented were successful. The most successful kind of representative was a social worker (58 per cent success rate) with solicitors and friends or relatives trailing behind (37 per cent and 29 per cent respectively). Only about 17 per cent of the total had any form of representation.[19]

Representation is important where the tribunal is arbitrating between state and citizen; but it is equally important in disputes between two inherently unequal classes of citizen, for example, landlords versus tenants, employers versus employees. In such cases one side is much more likely to be represented than the other. The problem aggravates the difficulties facing people in need who lack the skills necessary to claim even the meagre benefits that the state provides.

5. Tribunals cannot achieve "justice" in areas of policy which are themselves unjust or founded on muddled thinking. With the best will in the world, rent tribunals could not be expected to clear up the mess that successive governments have made of housing policy and rent control legislation.

The Parliamentary Commissioner

The Ombudsman approach began in Sweden in 1809; it spread to Finland in 1919, to Denmark in 1954 and to both New Zealand and Norway in 1962. In 1967 the office of Parliamentary Commissioner for Administration was set up in Britain to deal with complaints of "maladministration" (see below) against central government departments. Although the PCA is often called "the Ombudsman" he is a pale shadow of his Scandinavian namesakes who can, on their own initiative, inquire into virtually every field of government activity and even initiate prosecutions against corrupt officials and ministers.

The PCA deals only with complaints referred to him by MPs; many critics consider that his main weakness is his lack of powers to deal directly with the general public. Moreover, his jurisdiction extends only to specified central government departments (excluding public corporations, the armed services, personnel matters in the civil service and, until recently, local government and the National Health Service). He is concerned with "maladministration". When the Bill setting up the PCA was being debated in the House of Commons, Mr Crossman defined maladministration as, "bias, neglect, inattention, delay, incompetence, ineptitude, perversity, turpitude, arbitrariness and so on".

The PCA can examine all official documents except Cabinet papers and his ultimate weapon is publicity, though it is doubtful whether existing publicity is very effective. He reports to Parliament through a Select Committee, very much along the lines of the Comptroller and Auditor General and the Public Accounts Committee.

So far his achievements have been slight. In his first five years over half the complaints referred to him were outside his jurisdiction; but in about 12 per cent of the cases he investigated he found elements of injustice caused by maladministration. On close inspection, however, most of these turn out to have been minor matters; very often over-worked tax officials suddenly presenting large bills for the payment of past tax after the taxpayer has been underassessed in previous years, plus plenty of instances of discourtesy or failure to answer letters. In some cases the PCA has managed to persuade departments to make *ex gratia* payments, but he cannot force them to provide a remedy; all he can do is try to achieve a result by diplomacy and then pub-licise the case if he is unsuccessful.

The one case of real substance concerned some British servicemen who had been detained in the Nazi concentration camp at Sachsen-hausen.[20] Eventually the PCA managed to get these men com-pensated after the Foreign Office had refused their claim on the basis of what the PCA called "partial and largely irrelevant information". This case is worth studying as a nice illustration of the problems surrounding the Commissioner's position in relation to conventions about ministerial responsibility.

On balance the office of PCA has been neither a spectacular suc-cess nor a dismal failure. Since October 1973 the PCA (now Mr Cyril Clothier, QC) has been doubling as National Health Service Commis-sioner; here he can receive complaints directly from the public, but he only has jurisdiction when other avenues of complaint have been exhausted. The "ombudsman" model has also been imported into local government by the Local Government Act 1974. The three English local government commissioners generally receive complaints via elected councillors; this seems self-defeating given that the object is to allow independent investigation into complaints against councillors. The role of the latter in local government is quite different from the role of backbench MPs vis-à-vis the executive in central government.

The government's unwillingness to allow direct access stems largely from a feeling that this would subvert the established role of MPs and local councillors in dealing with public complaints; this seems highly unrealistic. One instance where an ombudsman has worked very well has been the "Complaints Commissioner" who has been operating in the context of local government in Northern Ireland since 1969 and who receives complaints direct from the public. The shortcomings of the PCA have been thoroughly and constructively reviewed by a committee of *Justice*, whose report, aptly entitled *Our Fettered Ombudsman*, appeared in 1977.

Towards an administrative court?
A report by "Justice" in 1961[21] was one of the first shots in the battle to set up the PCA; it also recommended that an all-purpose tribunal should be set up to coordinate the existing tribunal system and to plug some of the gaps in it. Some opponents of the PCA idea have strongly supported the establishment of a fully-fledged system of administrative law, administered by special courts, as on the Continent.

When the Labour Government's White Paper, foreshadowing the setting up of the PCA, was published in 1965, the Inns of Court Conservative and Unionist Association counterattacked with a pamphlet called *Let Right be Done*, in which they advocated grafting an "Administrative Commission" on to the Privy Council to provide a comprehensive body of administrative remedies. A Fabian Tract published in December 1973[22] advocated a single "social court" to replace tribunals, backed up by a special social division of the Court of Appeal.

One of the most realistic excursions into this field was another Justice report, *Administration Under Law*, published in 1971. This suggests the enactment by Parliament of a number of principles of "good administration" (a sort of mini-Bill of Rights, see chapter 7) including an obligation to give due notice of proceedings and a full opportunity to be heard; and obligation upon all public authorities to give reasoned decisions and to notify them promptly to those affected. Such principles should, it says, be enforced by a new administrative division of the High Court, equipped with a more flexible armoury of remedies, including the power to award compensation for administrative transgressions.[23]

This plan certainly seems to provide a sensible means of retaining the best features of the existing system while putting the machinery of administrative law on a more coherent and rational footing. It is sometimes suggested that we have a straight choice between keeping our ombudsman and setting up an administrative court. This is not the case; the French, who have a well-developed system of administrative courts headed by the *Conseil d'État*, have set up the office of *Médiateur*, which is a variant on the ombudsman theme.

In Britain there can be little doubt that our system of administrative remedies is a mess; indeed, it is hardly accurate to call it a "system" at all. The time has come for a drastic review. In 1969 the Law Commission[24] recommended the setting up of a Royal Commission to consider citizens' rights and remedies against the state. This proposal has so far been studiously ignored by successive governments. Meanwhile there has been some incremental change: in 1977 important changes were announced both in the working of Supplementary Benefit Appeal Tribunals[25] and in the cumbersome procedures for obtaining redress against the administration in the courts.[26] And, since the mid-1970s, the courts themselves have been very active. Thus in *Congreve* v *the Home Office*[27] they held that the Home Secretary had acted *ultra vires* in purporting to revoke television licences prudently purchased in advance of an announced increase in the fee. In the *Tameside* case[28] a Labour Minister of Education was held to have acted unlawfully in issuing a statutory directive to a Conservative-controlled local authority which had reversed its Labour predecessors' scheme for comprehensive secondary schooling. In 1980 a Conservative Secretary for Social Services was held to have exceeded his power in issuing a directive transferring the functions of the Lewisham Area Health Authority to a body of appointed Commissioners on the grounds that the Authority had not complied with the government's cash-limits on expenditure.

These and many other recent cases remind us (*a*) that even ministers are not above the law and (*b*) that even in the absence of a Bill of Rights (see chapter 7) the courts can be part of the battleground of politics. Whether an interventionist judiciary, accountable in practice only to itself, is a healthy feature of a democracy such as ours is very much another question.

6 The Law and Freedom of Expression

> But what is Freedom? Rightly understood, a universal licence to be good.
>
> HARTLEY COLERIDGE

It is often boasted that Britain is a "free country". Clearly this cannot be taken to mean that everyone in Britain is legally free to do as he or she wishes. We are free only to do what is not legally forbidden. But as we have seen in chapter 1 we know where we stand if there is a framework of order provided by a legal system. In Britain the will of the state can be enforced only through laws passed by Parliament and applied and interpreted by the courts.

Freedom, like morality, is a relative thing. Concepts such as "freedom of speech" and "freedom of assembly" are an important part of our political culture but, looked at more closely, rhetorical phrases like these turn out to be an imperfect reflection of an amorphous set of individual beliefs about how things *ought* to be – beliefs which, in the nature of things, will differ from person to person and from generation to generation. One person will interpret "freedom of speech" to confer a completely unrestricted right to speak or publish anything; others will allow exceptions of various kinds to prevent the propagation of what they consider to be socially or morally dangerous. The borderline between "liberty" (a word which produces favourable responses in most people, even if their conceptions of its meaning differ widely) and dangerous "licence" is ambiguous, subjective and ever-fluctuating.

In legal terms the boundaries are even less distinct in this country than elsewhere because, as we shall see in the next chapter, we have no written constitution and no Bill of Rights (though we do sub-

scribe to the European Convention on Human Rights). Judges in
the United States, unlike those in Britain, can enforce constitutional
rights of free speech. This is not the same as saying that British law
does not protect free speech, merely that such a right, in so far as it
exists, is to be found in particular laws and in the attitudes of legislators, judges and policemen.

Free expression and democratic government

An essential ingredient of any political system claiming to be
"democratic" is effective lines of communication between governors
and governed. Perfect equality, in the sense of everyone having
equal resources and an equal voice in government is Utopian; but
advocates of representative democracy set great store by the necessity for free and open debate on public issues and by the freedom
allowed to different groups to express their views, even if those views
are at variance with those of the ruling establishment.

A sign of maturity and stability (perhaps even of complacency) in
a state is when opponents of the *status quo* are allowed a public
platform for their beliefs. On the face of it, freedom of expression
appears well developed in this country; the range of interest groups
and minority political parties seems endless, the media are not
answerable to the government[1] (even if they are accused of being too
"establishment minded"), and demonstrations and public meetings
are almost an everyday occurrence, with only isolated reports of
serious disruption. Satire directed at public figures is accepted as a
part of everyday life; *Private Eye* is nowadays almost as accepted as
The Times.

But what is the reality behind this appearance of liberty, tolerance
and tranquillity, and what are the legal and other constraints on
"freedom of expression"? The subject is vast and complex and the
reader is advised to turn for more details to H. Street, *Freedom, the
Individual and the Law* and to F. Stacey, *A New Bill of Rights for
Britain* (see Bibliography). Let us begin with a brief look at the
operation of censorship in the various branches of the mass media.

Theatre censorship

The Theatres Act 1968 ended the role of the Lord Chamberlain
in censoring stage plays; the Act followed the report of a parliamentary joint committee set up to consider the subject. Under the old

system the Lord Chamberlain's office customarily placed firm restrictions, not just on matters of sex or violence, but also upon the portrayal of public figures and persons recently dead, not to mention God and members of the Royal Family. Shows as harmless as *Jesus Christ Superstar* and *Crown Matrimonial* (on the abdication of Edward VIII) would never have been allowed.

The 1968 Act puts plays on a similar footing to published books, that is they come under the same rules laid down in the Obscene Publications Act 1959 (see below). Those prosecuted can now plead that the performance as a whole was for the public good, even if parts of it are thought obscene. There are special provisions against incitement to racial hatred and provocation of public disturbances. Offensive and inaccurate references to individuals can be the subject of an action for libel.

There can be little doubt that the change has had a healthily liberating effect on the English theatre. There have been a few prosecutions, and a few productions that have been in dubious taste, but on balance the benefits have been considerable. In any case, it by no means follows because something is in bad taste, obscene or immoral, that it should be banned by law.

The cinema

Celluloid is highly inflammable stuff; early films were made of this dangerous material and in 1909 an Act was passed requiring local authorities, either on their own account or by delegating the task to the local justices, to license cinemas in the interests of public safety. The authorities assumed the power to make stipulations about the content of films shown, and the courts upheld their right to do so. In the interests of uniformity, the film industry set up the British Board of Film Censors. This body is not a government agency but a "Quango", which maintains links with the Home Office.

In practice most local authorities allow themselves to be guided by the certificates issued by the Board, though some authorities (notably the GLC) have occasionally allowed films to be shown after the BBFC has refused to grant a certificate.

The laws of obscenity and defamation apply to films; in practice, however, a prosecution for obscenity is most unlikely to succeed against a film carrying a BBFC certificate, though in May 1974 the Lord Chief Justice ruled that a prosecution could be brought against the distributor of the film *Last Tango in Paris*, which had been exhibited under an X-certificate for more than a year (he was later acquitted). Those who disapprove of censorship must disapprove of the BBFC; but, on the whole, in recent years, the Board has displayed a liberal and imaginative approach to its task. Their well-known categories, "U", "A", "AA" and "X" at least warn people what they are in for.

Broadcasting
Radio and television are the most intrusive of all the mass media in that they are present in nearly everyone's living rooms, and the constraints that apply to them tend therefore to be greater. Both the BBC and the IBA exercise internal self-censorship, though the legal basis of their duty to do so differs; the BBC's position derives originally from royal charter and its powers and obligations are set out in a licence issued by the Minister of Posts and Telecommunications. (In 1974 this Ministry was absorbed into the Department of Industry.) The Minister is empowered to issue directives to the BBC about the content of its broadcasts. The position of the IBA is defined in Acts of Parliament; the Authority itself does not provide broadcasts but subcontracts the task to companies (London Weekend, Granada, etc). The Acts make certain stipulations about programme content, and the Authority must exercise supervision over the programmes put out by the contractors. Again, the Minister is empowered to issue directives. Both bodies are required to maintain quality and good taste in their programmes; in the case of BBC this derives from a ministerial directive, in the case of IBA the obligation is statutory.[2]

Of particular interest to students of politics are the rules which require a fair balance in programmes that are politically controversial. The IBA has a statutory duty to ensure that such a balance is achieved; the BBC's position is somewhat less clearcut, though it has entered into an arrangement with the parties whereby the Opposition is given the automatic right to reply to any ministerial broadcast which has a controversial content.

Party political broadcasts as such are governed by special rules; politicians have done nothing to enhance their popularity by insisting that such broadcasts are screened simultaneously on all three television channels at peak viewing time. Time for such broadcasts is shared out among the parties in proportion to the votes cast for them in the preceding general election – an arrangement which works against new or re-emerging parties.

Many politicians seem to fear that broadcasting and television have replaced the House of Commons as the main forum for political debate. Certainly there is a tendency to judge political leaders as much by their adroitness under interrogation by Sir Robin Day as by their skill in parliamentary debate. One obvious answer seems to be "if you can't beat them, join them" – televise Parliament. But, at the time of writing, politicians have not come round to accepting this idea, though regular radio broadcasts of Commons debates began in 1978. Certainly political leaders are increasingly sensitive about alleged bias on BBC and ITV. Each party thinks it is discriminated against when in power. Perhaps it is in the nature of "news" that the Opposition always appears more interesting.

The press

Our attitudes towards newspapers tends to be conditioned by the newspapers themselves. We receive many of our opinions, as well as a substantial proportion of our knowledge, from journalists who have a tendency to inflate their own importance in the scheme of things and to foster a fundamental belief that "freedom of the press" is something akin to holy writ. There have been notorious instances of press barons meddling in politics, to the fury of politicians: in 1931, for example, Stanley Baldwin, incensed by Lord Rothermere's efforts to interfere with his job of forming a cabinet, complained that the newspaper proprietors were seeking "power without responsibility, the prerogative of the harlot through the ages".

The press is not politically neutral, and it is not particularly desirable that it should be; the danger lies in the frequency with which political judgments are dressed up as hard facts. Some newspapers display considerable hypocrisy in justifying "muck raking" stories about the private lives of public figures as being in the public interest. On the other hand they are often lazy in accepting press handouts issued by police, government, industry, etc, without attribution or checking. Occasionally there may be a conflict of loyalties when an editor is considering publishing a story which may antagonise an organisation on which a paper relies for advertising revenue.

Nevertheless, despite all objections, a free and independent press is one vital prerequisite of democracy. Newspapers should be in commercial competition with one another and not under state control, even though the price we must pay is an unhealthy journalistic pre-occupation with "scoops" and "exclusives".

The government does not censor newspapers except in wartime (the Communist *Daily Worker* was suppressed altogether in 1941), but the press is often accused of being "establishment minded", and journalists may have to be circumspect in handling stories which may lead to the drying up of potential sources of vital information. The whole edifice of political journalism is erected on a foundation of accredited lobby correspondents who have access to ministers and "inside" stories but are forbidden, on pain of losing their privileges, to name their sources.[3] Some newspaper proprietors have worked closely with politicians (for example, Lord Beaverbrook with Churchill). *The Times* used to have a semi-official status and was interpreted as such by foreign governments; during the 1930s, for instance, the Germans assumed that the pro-appeasement editorials of *The Times* were inspired by the British government – and they often were.[4] But it has now lost this status.

Following the report of the Royal Commission on the Press in 1949,[5] the Press Council was established in 1953 to maintain jour-nalistic standards and to deal with complaints against newspapers. This is a voluntary body, still with only a minority of members from outside Fleet Street. In recent years its chairman has been a distin-guished ex-judge or a front-rank lawyer. Since 1978 the chairman has been Patrick Neill, QC. The Council has done something to raise ethical standards in journalism; it has been very critical of such practices as paying vast sums for the memoirs of notorious public figures such as Christine Keeler and sundry criminals (including Donald Hume, the self-confessed murderer and Ronald Biggs, the Great Train Robber). Among its adjudications was one upholding complaints against Sunday newspapers for their irresponsible use of tape recordings and photographs taken in connection with the exposé of Lord Lambton's association with a prostitute. However, many newspapers have, with impunity, more or less ignored adverse adjudications by the Council and, as the Jeremy Thorpe trial showed, "cheque book journalism" continues unabated.

The greatest legal concern of newspapers is with the law of libel and with the rules relating to contempt of court, which prevent news-papers, to their frequent annoyance, from publishing material relating to legal proceedings while the latter are before the courts.

On one famous occasion the editor of the *Daily Mirror* was sent to prison for publishing highly prejudicial allegations against a man accused of murder before he had been tried. The law of contempt can operate to curb transgressions of a far less blatant kind than this. There is currently a debate about whether there should be a legal right of privacy which would, among other things, entitle people to protection against intrusive journalism.

Obscenity

The problem of defining something as "obscene" lies at the heart of the debate about law and morality outlined in chapter 2. Should people be allowed to choose for themselves whether to watch films or read books containing material which others consider highly offensive, or is the very existence of such material a threat to our social order? There is, moreover, a practical problem: the law has defined obscenity as meaning something having a "tendency to deprave and corrupt" those into whose hands it is likely to fall. But how can we measure corruption? Is it not possible to argue that a bookseller who purveys works depicting esoteric sexual activities is offering them to people who can be labelled, because of their taste for this kind of thing, as already "corrupt"?

The legal definition was laid down in a case decided in the nineteenth century[6] and has been perpetuated in subsequent legislation (see below); in that case the judge gave further clues to what he meant by explaining that the work in question "would suggest to the minds" of the reader "thoughts of a most impure and libidinous character". But Professor Street points out the difficulty:

When is a thought impure? Only when it relates to sexual passion? To normal sexual intercourse? In the marriage bed or outside? To perversions? Do books on sex in marriage corrupt or deprave? What degree of causal relationship must there be between the book and the sexual thought? Do we know when and how and to what extent the reading of a particular book will arouse sexual passions, either within itself or with the aid of other stimuli, and, if only with the aid of the latter, is this sufficiently causal? In any case, should the law concern itself with men's thoughts?[7]

The law in this area is very confused and the position was tellingly satirised by A.P. Herbert in one of his famous and fictitious

Uncommon Cases called "Is Homer Obscene?" – Presiding at the trial of the Headmaster of Eton for having on the school premises various Greek and Latin classics, allegedly of an obscene character, the chairman of the bench expressed his revulsion for

> the record of the alleged god, Zeus, whose habit it was to assume the shape of swans, bulls and other animals, and, thus disguised, to force his attentions upon defenceless females of good character. The case of the woman Leda, if it were published in the newspapers today, would arouse the indignation of every right-thinking Englishman . . .[8]

In 1959, following the recommendation of a parliamentary joint committee, Mr. Roy Jenkins successfully sponsored a Private Member's Bill which was enacted as the Obscene Publications Act 1959. This measure considerably improved the law on obscenity; although it retains the nineteenth-century definition, the Act makes it clear that the article in question must be "taken as a whole" – thereby ending the practice whereby the prosecution could read out juicy selections to the jury (by selective quotation it is not hard to make *The Bible* or *The Complete Works of Shakespeare* sound obscene). The most important innovation was section 4 which entitles the defence to call evidence to prove

> that publication of the article in question is justified as being for the public good on the ground that it is in the interests of science, literature, art or learning, or of other objects of general concern.

The Act was soon put to the test in the prosecution of Penguin Books for publishing D.H. Lawrence's *Lady Chatterley's Lover*. The defence called expert witnesses to testify to the book's literary merit, and the publishers were acquitted.

There have been a number of important prosecutions under the 1959 Act (amended in 1964). In 1971 the editors of the "underground" magazine *Oz* were prosecuted in respect of an edition to which school children had been invited to contribute; the trial was notable for the cavalier attitude adopted by the judge towards some of the expert defence witnesses and by the fact that substantial prison sentences were imposed on conviction. The convictions on most counts were quashed on appeal and the sentences reduced; but the Court of Appeal laid down the worrying proposition that, whereas a book must be considered as a whole, a magazine can be considered item by item. This appears to run counter to the spirit of the 1959 Act.

The Act has undoubtedly brought about a welcome relaxation in the law of obscenity, which had hitherto operated against many works of genuine literary quality. Indeed it has become quite difficult in the last few years to persuade juries to convict. This fact has caused great concern to people like Lord Longford who was so appalled by the spectre of the "permissive society" that he set up his own private committee of inquiry which led to a large report on pornography published in 1973.

But those of liberal sentiments in this matter have not had it all their own way; there are still plenty of legal constraints. For example, the police can apply to magistrates for the power to seize allegedly obscene articles; the latter are then perused by the magistrates, who can order that they be forfeited. Although the defence can plead the "public good" in such cases, it is effectively deprived of the right of jury trial. Sometimes the police are overzealous or careless in what they seize; the reports of a case early in 1974 revealed that such untitillating material as *The Times Literary Supplement* had been taken, along with *Playboy*, *Mayfair*, etc. There is a suspicion that the police sometimes take much more than they ever intend to make the subject of a prosecution simply to cause maximum inconvenience to the bookseller concerned.

Other bits and pieces of legislation give further scope for prosecution, and deny any defence of public good. It is an offence to send indecent matter through the post. Customs officers are empowered to seize indecent items and their opinions of what is obscene are not always widely shared nor open to effective challenge. In February 1974 the publishers of *Men Only* were successfully prosecuted under the Customs and Excise Act 1952. The Vagrancy Acts, the Metropolitan Police Act, and numerous other old laws can be pressed into service in this context. And, if all else fails, the offender can always be indicted for conspiracy to corrupt public morals: this offence was resurrected in the *Ladies' Directory* case (see p. 18) and, more recently, when the publishers of the *International Times* were fined for including advertisements intended to facilitate contacts between male homosexuals, although homosexual behaviour by adults is no longer a criminal offence.[9]

Even many of those who favour liberalisation of the laws on obscenity would agree that people should not be *obliged* to witness things which they find distasteful; there has been a movement to strengthen and clarify the law relating to the public display of indecent material in the form of posters and public exhibitions. An inquiry chaired by Professor Bernard Williams reported in November 1979 that the law is a mess and that terms like "indecent" and "obscene" have outlived their usefulness. It proposed that pornographic books, films, etc. *should* be made available, but under strictly controlled conditions to ensure that young people were protected and that the general public would not be offended by offensive displays in shop windows or outside cinemas. Meanwhile the law remains an impenetrable jungle.[10]

Defamation and privacy
Someone whose character is damaged by a false statement can obtain damages for the torts of libel or slander. The defendant can get off the hook if he shows that his statement, however damaging, is substantially true. Some statements are "absolutely privileged" and cannot be the subject of a successful action, for example, statements made in Parliament or in the courts. Other categories of statement, such as newspaper reports of local authority proceedings, are subject to "qualified privilege" which means they are not actionable unless it can be shown that the maker of the statement was actuated by malice – a very hard thing to prove. From the journalist's point of view the most important defence to a libel action is that the statement, although in fact untrue, was fair comment on a matter of public interest; this covers, for example, unfavourable book reviews and newspaper reports on the activities of people in public life.

The law of defamation is very complicated and contains many loopholes. Libel actions are very costly and fall into a category of proceedings for which it is not possible to get legal aid. Apart from the cost, a plaintiff is often deterred from bringing an action by the fact that, even if he wins, he may suffer further unwelcome publicity. And a successful action may bring scant return by way of damages because in recent years the courts have placed heavy restrictions upon the award of "punitive damages" over and above the amount thought proper to compensate the plaintiff for his loss of reputation.

So, although newspapermen often grumble that defamation is an affront to "freedom of the press", the law works, on the whole, on their side. Editors often find it worth while to take calculated risks with dubious stories. Indeed, there is a respectable body of opinion that considers that newspapers enjoy too much freedom; in addition to cheque-book journalism and the temptation to sail close to the wind in matters of libel, there are occasional incidents of gross invasions of privacy by journalists – of photographers perched in trees with telephoto lenses, of newsmen who enter people's homes by pretending to be tradesmen, of journalists who pester a man's friends, neighbours and even his children in search of personal information.

No doubt this kind of journalism is the exception rather than the rule; and there are others who have been making a living out of invasions of privacy. In recent years there have been a number of cases where private detectives have proved able, with alarming ease, to breach the security arrangements of government departments, banks and even police records departments, to obtain private information about peoples' tax records, their bank balances, their claims on social security and their criminal records. People have begun to ask why we do not institute a legal right to personal privacy such as exists in a number of other countries. Concern has increased with the ever-growing use of automatic data storage and retrieval and the development of sophisticated "bugging" devices.

In 1970 a report by Justice[11] recommended legislation to give a civil remedy for invasion of privacy. Mr Brian Walden, MP, incorporated these proposals in a Private Member's Bill. The Government objected to the Bill, but it set up a committee of inquiry under the chairmanship of Mr Kenneth Younger to examine the problem of privacy; the terms of reference excluded public bodies, with the exception of the broadcasting organisations and the universities.

The Committee's report appeared in 1972[12] and, with two members dissenting, it rejected the proposal for a general legal right of privacy, on the rather unconvincing ground that the courts would find it difficult to apply such a law. It did propose the introduction of criminal penalties for carrying out surreptitious surveillance using a technical device (bugging); and it recommended civil remedies for unlawful surveillance and for the publication of information unlawfully acquired. The Committee also proposed for parliamentary consideration that private detectives should be licensed, that the Press Council should increase the proportion of its membership who are non-journalists and that the Government should set up a standing commission to review the use of personal information stored in computer data banks.

The Race Relations Acts

The Race Relations Act 1965 made it unlawful to discriminate against any person on the grounds of colour, race or nationality in public places like hotels, cinemas and restaurants or in public transport; it established the Race Relations Board to conciliate in matters of alleged racial discrimination. The Race Relations Act 1968 substantially amended the 1965 Act, making it illegal to practice discrimination in the provisions of goods and services and in matters of employment or housing.

Section 6 of the 1965 Act makes it a criminal offence to incite people to racial hatred either by distributing pamphlets etc, or by using inflammatory words at a public meeting. This section has led to the successful prosecution of, among others, Colin Jordan, the British National Socialist, and Michael X, the self-styled Black Power leader. Nevertheless Section 6 gives rise to problems; it is drafted in such a way that it is not even necessary for the prosecution to show that an actual breach of the peace was likely to occur at the meeting in question.

There is also a difficult issue of principle. Democracy, as we have argued, requires that all shades of opinion should, within reason, be allowed the right of free expression; the criminal law should only set very broad limits upon what is permissible. Public policy rightly places a high premium on racial harmony, and the Race Relations Acts are directed to that end; but if we accept that in this case the end justifies the means, could we complain in principle if public policy led one day to laws which suppressed the expression of views favourable to (say) pacifism or communism?

Public meetings and demonstrations

Hand in hand with the assertion that people should be allowed to speak or write as they think fit goes the belief that people should be free to hold meetings and demonstrations to make their views known. How does the law operate in this area?

Contrary to popular belief, there is no absolute legal right of freedom of assembly. The holding of meetings in public places, even the cherished right to speak at Speakers' Corner in Hyde Park, is subject to regulation by bye-laws; and those participating must conform to the laws about race relations and public order. An orderly procession on the public highway is within the law, until it crosses the invisible barrier which turns it into criminal obstruction.

The Public Order Act 1936 empowers the police to regulate or

even (subject to local authority and ministerial approval) ban pro-
cessions and demonstrations that seem likely to provoke disorder.
Section 5 of the Act makes it a criminal offence to use insulting
behaviour at a public meeting whereby a breach of the peace is
likely to ensue; it has been held that the speaker is still liable even if it
turns out that his audience consists of rowdies determined to cause a
disturbance whatever he says. As we have seen, it is also an offence
to incite to racial hatred.

   This is an area where restraint and good sense matter more than
legal rules. The authorities have plenty of powers to interfere with
meetings and demonstrations; if they cannot find a statutory power
then there is always the common law catch-all of "conspiracy", as
Mr Peter Hain discovered when he was convicted of conspiring to
disrupt sporting events in furtherance of his campaign to stop the
Springbok Rugby Tour in 1970. In practice, however, the discretion
to take steps against demonstrations is, for the most part, used with
good sense. Considering the number and scale of mass demonstrations in this country over the years it is remarkable how few really
serious clashes have taken place. But there have been some notable
instances of heavy-handedness by the police (for example, in connection with some of the CND demonstrations in the early 1960s
and the clashes in Southall in 1979). There has been much debate on
how far we should go in preserving "free speech" for groups like
the National Front who promote racial intolerance. A green paper on
the Public Order Act appeared in April 1980, but the real issue goes
far deeper.

Official secrecy[13]

It is all very well our being able to claim a right of free speech, but
our ability to exercise that right depends upon our having something
worthwhile to speak about. Meaningful political debate is impossible
unless we have access to information about what is happening in the
corridors of power; representative democracy has little point to it
unless there is a continuous dialogue between governors and
governed. In recent years there has been a growing concern that
public bodies in Britain are much too reticent about their activities.
Part of the disease can be attributed to the all-embracing nature of
the Official Secrets Acts.

   The first Official Secrets Act was passed in 1889 following cases in
which civil servants had leaked highly confidential information (in
one case the text of a secret treaty had been published in a news-

paper) and it was found that they had committed no criminal offence as the law then stood. The 1889 Act was found to have too many loopholes and in 1911, at which time there was mounting concern about German espionage, a new Act was passed: it went through the Commons in a single day. The provisions of the 1911 Act were extended by a new measure enacted in 1920.

Section 1 of the 1911 Act is aimed at spies; in principle, there has been little criticism of this aspect of the legislation. The real problem derives from Section 2, captioned "wrongful communication, etc, of information". This section makes it an offence carrying a maximum penalty of two years imprisonment to communicate any official information to an "unauthorised" person or to receive any official document knowing, or having reasonable grounds to believe, that it was communicated in contravention of the Act. Section 8 of the Act requires all prosecutions to be authorised by the Attorney-General.

It will be noted that Section 2 says nothing about spying, nor does it require the prosecution to prove that positive harm has resulted from the leakage of information. All kinds of people in public service – civil servants (senior and junior), politicians, prison officers and postmen – are affected by its provisions; in theory they are open to prosecution for the most harmless tittletattle relating to their work. In practice, the number of prosecutions has amounted to only about one a year since the last war, but the inhibiting threat of liability to prosecution is what matters. Some of those prosecuted deserve all they got, for example, the postman who was sent to prison for offering criminals information to enable them to rob a post office. But several of the cases have arisen out of the sort of irresponsibility which, if the accused had been employed in a private concern, would, at most, have led to his being dismissed: in one case a clerk at Somerset House was sent to prison for prematurely disclosing the contents of wills to a newspaperman.

The Fulton Report on the Civil Service emphasised the importance of "open decisions openly arrived at" and called for a review of the Official Secrets Acts. The Labour Government responded with a rather smug White Paper,[14] congratulating itself on the increased use of Green Papers etc as an aid to public debate and claiming that the requirement of the Attorney-General's consent to prosecution is an adequate safeguard. The latter proposition is dubious; in terms of justice being *seen* to be done in circumstances which often have political overtones it is hardly satisfactory to vest the decision to prosecute in a man who sits on the Government front bench in the House of Commons.

In 1970 the Conservatives came into office pledged to review official secrecy. Shortly afterwards came the much publicised *Sunday Telegraph* prosecution in which a number of people were acquitted of charges relating to publication in a newspaper of a confidential report on the Nigerian Civil War; in that case the trial judge said some very scathing things about Section 2.

A government inquiry was set up under the chairmanship of Lord Franks. In its Report, published in 1972,[15] the Committee found that Section 2 was "a mess"; it was a "catch-all", ambiguous and fickle in its operation. The Report recommended the repeal of the section and its replacement by an entirely new Official Information Act, designed to narrow down the categories of information covered; people should no longer be liable to prosecution merely for receiving leaked information.

The philosophy behind official secrets legislation is essentially negative, and bound up with ideas about ministerial responsibility which are fast becoming out of date. Ways of plugging leaks are not combined with means of ensuring that officials and politicians have a legal *duty* to act openly and reveal information; Swedish officials can be prosecuted for *concealing* official information when asked for it, though Swedish law does forbid leakage of confidential items in fields like defence, and places strict controls upon the revelation of private information about individuals. The Franks Committee touched on the question of introducing a legal right of public access to information but dismissed it as being outside its terms of reference. The last Labour government promised in October 1974 "to replace the Official Secrets Act by a new measure to put the burden on public authorities to justify witholding information". This rash promise was never kept, though in July 1977 the Head of the Civil Service told all departments to proceed on the working assumption that background material on policy decisions would be published – an exhortation which yielded very little in the way of material which would not have appeared anyway. At the end of its period of office the Callaghan government, shamed into action by a private Member's Bill on open government, produced a very negative green paper on the subject.[16]

Meanwhile it had undertaken to implement Franks (with minor modifications) and published a white paper to this effect.[17] At one point the then Home Secretary, Mr Rees, spoke of replacing the "blunderbuss" of Section 2 with a new "armalite rifle". Critics were quick to point out that armalite rifles have a lethal purpose; the one great virtue of the present legislation is that its defects make the government hesitant to prosecute under it. A recent fiasco was in November 1978 when three defendants were convicted after a long and costly trial of offences arising out of magazine articles about the Government's secret communications headquarters; the defendants were conditionally discharged and the case gave even wider publicity to the "secrets" involved. In the end the Government's Bill to replace Section 2 fell at the 1979 dissolution. The Thatcher government introduced a similar measure, but later had second thoughts (following the Blunk security scandal) and withdrew it.

One final issue which is of relevance both to State security and to individual privacy is the practice of "tapping" people's telephones and intercepting their mail. Following the Birkett report of 1957 safeguards were devised, requiring warrants to be approved personally by the Home Secretary or the Secretary of State for Scotland. Since 1957 a lot has changed: electronic technology has become more sophisticated; desperate measures have had to be taken to combat terrorism in Northern Ireland; in 1978 the European Court of Justice ruled that governments must provide effective safeguards.

Suspicions have grown that tapping is carried out on a large scale outside the spirit and even the letter of the Birkett guidelines. In April 1980 the Thatcher government published a white paper explaining how those guidelines operate today (though this did *not* cover Northern Ireland)[18]; the Government announced as an added safeguard that a senior judge (Lord Diplock) would be asked to carry out a continuing review of the procedures. This is welcome so far as it goes, and it cannot be denied that tapping has resulted in successful police action against terrorists, robbers and drug smugglers. At the same time one cannot avoid the suspicion that the safeguards are cosmetic and that a lot of routine tapping (and "bugging" – not discussed at all in the white paper) goes on without ministers knowing, or wanting to know, very much about it. It is hard to imagine any safeguards in an area so entwined with State security (as perceived by the authorities) being really convincing: who, in the last analysis, will guard the guardians? Perhaps the European Court (see above) may yet have the last word.

7 Prosecution and Defence

Liberty, too, must be limited in order to be possessed.

EDMUND BURKE

A policeman's lot is not a happy one.

W.S. GILBERT

Police and government

Police are intermediaries between state and citizen and a visible manifestation of governmental authority. In their hands rests the responsibility for the day to day application of the criminal law and the maintenance of order; from the citizen's point of view, the impact of the criminal law may hinge on differing prosecution policies between one police authority and the next. Policemen are instruments of public order, but there is much to be said for keeping them apart from politics and government. At times of peace and stability this may be feasible, but what happens if there is civil disorder? Where do the police stand in a national strike or in a violent political demonstration or, for that matter, in a quarrel between a white man and a black man? The reply that the police must be "neutral" raises more questions than it answers.

Police forces outside London are administered by chief constables answerable to local police authorities; the Home Secretary is the police authority for the Metropolitan force. The control exercised by the central government is complex and ambiguous. The situation is summarised as follows by Geoffrey Marshall:

The Home Secretary has . . . in some sense a responsibility for law and order throughout the country. He has statutory power to frame certain types of regulation for the administration of police forces, to act as an appeal authority in disciplinary matters and to approve the appointment of chief constables. Fifty per cent of approved local authority expenditure on police comes from an exchequer grant which is conditional *inter alia* on the Secretary of State's being satisfied that the area in question is effectively policed. For this purpose a force of inspectors is maintained.[1]

The constitutional status and administrative organisation of the police was reviewed by a Royal Commission which reported in 1962[2] and decisively rejected the setting up of a nationally run, unified police force. Important changes were made by the Police Act 1964, which, among other things, revised the machinery for reviewing complaints against the police.

Complaints against the police

Until the Police Act 1964 a serious complaint by a member of the public against a police officer was invariably investigated by the chief constable of the officer's own force. The 1964 Act not only required more systematic recording of complaints but also provided that a chief constable may, and *must* if so directed by the Home Secretary, request the chief constable of another force to conduct the investigation. In fact hardly any such directives have been issued by successive Home Secretaries and only a tiny minority of complaints is subjected to outside scrutiny. The chief constable must refer reports of all investigations to the Director of Public Prosecutions, unless he is satisfied that no criminal offence has been committed.

These were small improvements on former practice, but in terms of justice being *seen* to be done it is still highly unsatisfactory to let the police act as judges in their own cause even if (as many policemen claim) investigations tend to err on the side of harshness against officers who bring their force into disrepute.

Various proposals have been put forward for independent ombudsmen or tribunals to deal with complaints. Such proposals were strongly resisted by the Police Federation and by senior police officers, led by the then Metropolitan Police Commissioner, Robert Mark, who had fought his own campaign to root out police corruption. The Police Act 1976 made a modest change: a Police Complaints Board was set up, under the chairmanship of Lord Plowden, to act as an independent watchdog of police investigations, with a power in exceptional cases to set up its own disciplinary tribunal.

The Board's second annual report[3] showed that in 11,888 of 13,079 public complaints in 1978 the police had declined to take action: the Board recommended action in just 15 of these.

Of the complaints, 19 per cent alleged breaches of the Judges' Rules (see below) by policemen, 19 per cent alleged assaults, 17 per cent alleged incivility. Forty per cent were subsequently withdrawn. One relevant factor here is that (as an explanatory leaflet given to complainants points out) it may be open to an officer to bring a libel action if an allegation against him proves groundless. In October 1979 a police constable in Liverpool obtained £100 damages from a man who had claimed that the police were waging a vendetta against him in connection with alleged driving offences.

The criminal trial: "Adversary" versus "Inquisitorial"

It is a good idea at this point to consider some general characteristics of the criminal trial process. We will later encounter (see p. 139) Lord Devlin's strictures against the high cost of an "adversary" trial process in which (in criminal trials, though the adjective applies equally to civil proceedings) defence and prosecution fight things out between themselves, with the judge acting as impartial umpire, summing-up at the end. This is in contrast to "inquisitorial" systems that operate on the Continent where an examining magistrate (*juge d'instruction*) conducts an extensive preliminary investigation (in secret, to avoid prejudice) and recommends whether a suspect should be brought to trial. Readers who have seen the film *Z*, or read Camus's novel *The Outsider* will be familiar with this kind of procedure. At the trial itself the judge plays a major part in examining witnesses, and he retires with the jury.

There is something to be said for both practices. The big complaint about the inquisitorial system is that suspects spend long periods in custody – though this is no less true of our system. Many of the basic deficiencies of the English process of criminal trial stem from the ritualised gamelike quality of the proceedings, which seem to place almost as much emphasis on the niceties of tactics and intricate rules of procedure and evidence as upon getting at the truth. At present the rules are deliberately weighted in favour of the accused (though it does not always work out that way); there is, as we shall see, a move to shift the balance. But whether this could be done without lawyers being willing to contemplate a substantial movement away from the adversary system of trial seems very doubtful.

The process of prosecution

Anyone can initiate a prosecution, though in practice nearly all prosecutions are at the instigation of the police. The Director of Public Prosecutions (DPP), appointed by the Home Secretary and acting under the general direction of the Attorney-General, prosecutes in a small proportion of exceptionally serious or difficult cases and is available to give advice to the police on prosecution policy. The degree of coordination exercised by the DPP is very limited, and the policies of different police forces in deciding which offences to prosecute may vary widely.[4]

In crown courts the job of presenting the prosecution's case is entrusted to counsel, briefed on behalf of the Crown. A high proportion of prosecutions in magistrates' courts are undertaken by police officers; in many instances the prosecuting officer may be both advocate and prosecution witness in the same case. (Some police forces conduct their prosecutions through solicitors.)

The adversary trial process is based on a confrontation between two sides, each trying to balance a duty to the courts against a duty to its own client. The prosecution is there, at least in theory, to help the court arrive at the truth, not to secure a conviction at all costs. It seriously undermines this principle when the police are responsible for investigating the case, for deciding whether or not to prosecute, and then for presenting the case in court. The police are committed to the view that the accused is guilty so how can they (or even their solicitors) claim to be dispassionate? The defects of the present system are summarised in a Justice report on *The Prosecution Process in England and Wales*, published in 1970:

(a) It confuses two quite distinct and disparate functions and responsibilities, namely the vigorous investigation of crime: and the cool, careful objective assessment of the whole of the evidence and probabilities needed for a correct decision as to whether a prosecution should be started or, if started, continued.

(b) It offends against the principle that the prosecution should be – and should be plainly seen to be–independent, impartial and fair: concerned only with the pursuit of truth and not with winning or losing.

The report cites with approval the Scottish system of "procurators fiscal", the latter being qualified lawyers appointed by the Lord Advocate (Scottish equivalent of the Attorney-General) and responsible for initiating and conducting prosecutions in all but the most trivial cases; they operate independently from the police. The system of procurators fiscal is something that we might well import from Scotland – along with the duty solicitor scheme (see p. 153).

Arrest and interrogation: the Judges' Rules
Every citizen has the power to arrest someone committing a serious offence, but the police have powers over and above those available to members of the public. Public-spirited people (including store detectives) who effect "citizens' arrests" must be very sure of their ground if they want to avoid the risk of a successful civil action for false arrest. Warrants authorising arrests are issued by magistrates only to policemen. The latter also possess various statutory stop and search powers in respect of some offences like possession of drugs which would otherwise be "non-arrestable"; and the existence of a substantial number of local Acts means that police powers vary between one place and another.

The average citizen is ignorant of his basic rights. For example, few people seem to be aware that they are not obliged to accompany a policeman to the police station to answer questions unless they are placed under arrest. But, as Professor Street points out, the police seem to have very little difficulty in persuading people to forego their right to refuse:

The witness will recognise his public duty to aid detection of crime by giving the police all possible assistance. The innocent suspect will welcome the chance to clear himself. Even the guilty may see some advantage in trying to convince the police of his innocence; and in due course the jury may draw unfavourable conclusions from the accused's refusal to give a statement to the police. It may be doubted, too, whether the average citizen realizes that the police have no compulsive power; and one can hardly expect the police to make their task harder by prefacing every invitation to come to the police station with the express intimation that the citizen may please himself whether he accepts.[5]

This nicely illustrates the fact that a lot of authority is based ultimately upon bluff and misapprehension.

Policemen have to steer a difficult course between letting "too many" criminals get away with their misdeeds, while safeguarding the rights of the innocent; society asks the police to be efficient but forbids police officers from employing "unfair" tactics. Many policemen believe that the safeguards against the risk of convicting the innocent greatly undermine their effectiveness in bringing criminals to justice.

Nowhere are these problems more acute than in regard to rules governing police interrogation of suspects. These are not set out in an Act of Parliament but in the so-called Judges' Rules, promulgated by High Court Judges in 1906 and substantially amended in 1964; they were drawn up following incidents in Birmingham in 1906 where one judge criticised a policeman for having cautioned a prisoner and another judge censured an officer for not having done so. They require a policeman, at the point when it becomes clear that a person being questioned is likely to be charged with an offence, and again when he is actually charged, to caution him in the following words: "You are not obliged to say anything unless you wish to do so but what you say may be put into writing and given in evidence."[6] The Rules also cover the recording of statements made by the accused (the statements must be voluntary and given without prompting) and require that the accused must be given "reasonable" access to solicitor or friends. Although statements obtained by force or by the offer of improper inducement (such as making promises that charges will be dropped) may be inadmissible as evidence in court, proving this may be a matter of the accused's word against that of one or more policemen.

The Judges' Rules are not much of a safeguard and the police themselves regard them with considerable irritation. They see it as an absurdity that, when the prisoner is blurting out his guilty secrets, a policeman must stop him and tell him he need say no more. It galls them that, with the investigation of a crime reaching its triumphant climax, they must wait while the accused summons a glib-tongued lawyer who may get him off the hook on a legal "technicality".

There can be no doubt that the Rules are "bent" every day. Professor Street cites a letter written by an English policeman to an American friend in 1950:

All sorts of avoiding action are taken or otherwise the percentage of detections would be more than halved. You may have gathered that the said avoidance causes policemen to commit no little perjury in the box. . . . The ignorance of the Great British Public neutralizes the Judges' Rules. When we deal with an educated man who knows his rights, we have had it, unless we have outside evidence enough.[7]

Take, for example, the rule about statements being given without prompting. All too often it is impossible to imagine an inarticulate and semiliterate person in the dock having written a statement attributed to him, replete with long words and legal jargon. As Lord Devlin suggests, "the fault to be looked for today . . . is not the frame-up but the tendency to press interrogation too hard against a man believed to be guilty". A classic instance was the case of the mentally backward and illiterate Timothy Evans, hanged for murders committed (almost certainly) by his fellow-lodger, Christie. He was convicted largely on the basis of what we can now be almost sure were false confessions, presented by the police as having been dictated without prompting by Evans, but displaying a command of English far beyond his capabilities. The police "knew" he was guilty; tragically, they were wrong.[8]

Consider also the right to consult a lawyer. Michael Zander interviewed 134 men, all of whom had launched appeals to the criminal division of the Court of Appeal; he found that of fifty-seven who had asked the po є for access to a solicitor, 74 per cent had been refused. In one ca: t le dialogue allegedly went like this: "Who is your solicitor?" "I haven't got one." "Well, you can't contact one, can you?" Another prisoner who asked for a lawyer was told that he had been watching too many films.[9]

The right to legal advice both in the police station and in court (see chapter 9) is a crucial aspect of civil liberty. There are some, moreover, who consider that all interrogation should take place before magistrates (a view supported by Justice). Others, like the Criminal Law Revision Committee, consider that (lessons of Water-gate notwithstanding) police interrogations should be recorded on tape. It is to the report of the Criminal Law Revision Committee that we now turn.

The Report of the Criminal Law Revision Committee, 1972
The Committee's report, with the seemingly innocuous title of
Evidence (General), appeared in June 1972[10]; it contained proposals
for drastic revision of the machinery of criminal prosecution and
trial, which sparked off bitter controversy both inside and outside
the legal profession.

The Committee makes it clear from the outset that it favours
retention of the adversary trial system, of trial by jury and of the
summary jurisdiction of magistrates; it also believes that the burden
of proving guilt should rest, as at present, with the prosecution. Its
main concern is that the war against crime is being hampered by
unduly restrictive rules of evidence. The report argues that there is
now:

> a large and increasing class of sophisticated professional criminals
> who are not only highly skilful in organising their crimes and in
> the steps they take to avoid detection, but are well aware of their
> legal rights and use every possible means to avoid conviction if
> caught. These include refusal to answer questions by the police
> and the elaborate manufacture of false evidence.

It argues that the present rules of evidence are "a hindrance rather
than a help to justice". It criticises those who depict the trial process
as a game and suggests that legal fairness means the law being "such
as will secure as far as possible that the result of the trial is the right
one".

Its most important recommendations (and there are many others)
are as follows:

1. Abolition of the accused's right to remain silent under interrogation by the police. If an accused person fails to tell the police
   something which he could reasonably have mentioned and then
   raises it at his trial the court should be able to draw an adverse
   inference from his earlier silence.
2. Experiments should be made with methods of tape-recording
   police interrogations, but the Committee rejects proposals that
   interrogations should take place before magistrates.
3. Abolition of the practice of cautioning the suspect that he can
   remain silent (because it would obviously be inconsistent with
   recommendation 1); the report argues that, on the contrary, the

accused should be warned by the police that he may make things worse for himself by failing to mention any material fact.

4. The Judges' Rules in their present form should be replaced by administrative directives to the police by the Home Office.

5. Restriction upon the present right of an accused person to decline to give evidence on oath. The Committee suggests that in all trials the accused should be called upon formally to give evidence (so that the jury can see if the accused is choosing to keep quiet) and that the judge and prosecuting counsel should be empowered to draw unfavourable attention to the accused person's silence.

6. A number of changes in existing rules restricting the circumstances in which previous convictions of an accused person can be revealed in court; the proposals would, on balance, extend the circumstances in which previous convictions could be revealed.

7. Relaxation of the "hearsay" rule which, at present, greatly restricts the admissibility of evidence given by one witness about what some third party is supposed to have said.

8. Changes in the rules requiring some kinds of evidence to be corroborated by a second witness. Although these proposals would, on balance, operate against the accused, there is a favourable proposal that judges should warn juries of the danger of relying upon uncorroborated evidence of identity. (Some of the most notorious miscarriages of justice over the years have been based upon incorrect identification of accused persons by eye-witnesses.)

The most remarkable thing about the proposals was the near-unanimity of opposition to them. Barristers, solicitors, academics, an assortment of judges and journalists, plus sundry parliamentarians, all expressed hostile views. In the light of the proposals even ardent civil libertarians found hitherto unsuspected virtues in the *status quo*. It is unfortunate that so much of the report is based on conjecture and impression rather than on systematic observation and research. Rejection of the report led eventually to the setting up of a Royal Commission on Criminal Procedure (see Appendix 3).

Many of the criticisms focus on the abolition of the accused's right to remain silent during police interrogation and the separate, but related, issue of the accused being allowed to decline to give evidence in court. The former is widely denounced because of the added scope it gives to the police to put improper pressure upon suspects; critics argue that, even under the present system, there is much to be said for devices which can monitor police interrogation, and the Committee's proposals would make this even more essential

As to the right of remaining silent in court, this has been a feature of our legal system for many years; indeed, only since 1898 has the accused been allowed to be anything but silent. The United States Constitution, like many others, gives protection against self-incrimination; the Fifth Amendment says that no one "shall be compelled in any case to be a witness against himself". There is, however, a body of respectable opinion the other way. Jeremy Bentham could see no virtue in this protection; he depicted it as based on either "the old woman's reason" that "it is hard for a man to be obliged to incriminate himself", or on "the fox hunter's reason" that it is unsporting.

Probably the most succinct summary of the whole issue comes from the pen of Lord Devlin:

There is a school of thought which regards as purely sentimental the British reluctance to allow a man to convict himself out of his own mouth. They think it legitimate to get anything that can be got out of the suspect without ill-treatment. This is the inquisitorial system. To some extent we have it already. Into what is fundamentally an adversary system we have introduced an inquisitorial power, placing it in the hands of the police.

This hybrid device has worked tolerably well because we have demanded and largely obtained from the police a higher degree of impartiality than we have any right to expect and because it is subject to stringent control through the Judges' Rules. If the compromise has broken down, the answer is not to abolish the Rules and leave it all to the police. There are only two clean solutions. One is to withdraw the interrogatory power altogether, leaving the police in no better and no worse position than the plaintiff in a civil action. The other is to make it part of the legal process with an examining magistrate in charge of it.

If the State is going to impose upon the suspect the duty of submitting to questioning conducted in the hope of obtaining a confession or at least admissions that will help the prosecution, the State must ensure that the questioning is absolutely impartial, that the suspect is first told the nature of the case against him, that he has at this crucial stage the same sort of assistance as he needs at the trial and that there is a full record.

It is not insulting to the police to say that these requirements cannot be met in a police station. It is simply an application of the maxim that no one can be both prosecutor and judge. We tell the police to be ardent in the pursuit of crime. We cannot also demand that they should be detached in the assessment of guilt.[11]

Are too many criminals acquitted?

In a lecture delivered in November 1973, Sir Robert Mark, then Commissioner of the Metropolitan Police, said:

My own view is . . . that the proportion of those acquittals relating to those whom experienced police officers believe to be guilty is too high to be acceptable. That opinion is admittedly not universal. Many people, particularly lawyers, would disagree.

He went on to attribute part of the problem (as he saw it) to the "highly-paid forensic trickery" of defence lawyers, some of whom "are more harmful to society than the clients they represent". How much truth is there in the assertion, which also underlies the Report of the Criminal Law Revision Committee, that "too many" criminals are wrongly acquitted?

It is sometimes suggested that between 30 and 50 per cent of those pleading not guilty at trials on indictment (i.e. in crown courts) are acquitted. But this figure is meaningless unless we take into account the 70 per cent of accused persons who plead guilty; the overall acquittal rate is probably more of the order of 12 to 15 per cent. In magistrates' courts a much higher percentage plead guilty and acquittals are much rarer.

Moreover, critics often cite statistics which relate to the principal charge only. The prosecution may charge an accused with several offences so that if he escapes on the most serious he may still be convicted of something. It is hardly an "acquittal" when the jury finds a man not guilty of burglary but guilty of loitering with intent.

Research carried out in Oxford[12] into the outcome of 324 jury trials casts considerable doubt on the assumptions that are often made about acquittals. The researchers classified the 173 acquittals as follows:

58   cases where the judge directed the jury to acquit.

44   cases which seemed to be "policy prosecutions"; the police were trying to prove a point (for example, making it clear that all shoplifters would be prosecuted or reacting to a sudden outbreak of bicycle-stealing) rather than specifically to secure convictions.

20   cases where the prosecution case was so weak that a conviction cannot seriously have been expected. In some cases, for example, complainants had pressed the police to prosecute notwithstanding police misgivings about the wisdom of so doing.

 8   cases where the prosecution had a strong case but were let down by a poor performance from their witnesses.

28   cases where the accused's explanation of his conduct was sufficiently plausible to sow seeds of reasonable doubt.

15   "perverse" acquittals, though in some of these cases it was clear why the jury acted counter to the weight of evidence. In one case, for example, an Indian stall-holder had lashed out with a knife at a drunk who was abusing him; in law a plea of self-defence could not succeed, but it was clear that everyone in court was on his side.

The research also suggests a fallacy in the argument that "hardened" criminals are more likely to escape conviction; only 51 per cent of those acquitted had previous convictions (other than for minor motoring offences) compared with 81 per cent of those convicted.

Some critics may suggest that research carried out in Oxford can reveal very little about the wicked goings-on in big cities like London where "professional crime" is a booming industry. But in 1972 Michael Zander carried out a study of acquittals at the Old Bailey and the Inner London Crown Court, and confirmed the findings of the Oxford research. He found that only about 6 per cent of acquittals were "perverse" (compared with the Oxford figure of 9 per cent) and that most of these cases involved relatively minor offences.[13]

Such findings as these are by no means conclusive, but they do cast serious doubts on glib claims that too many criminals are escaping their just deserts. Moreover, even if we are presented with a carefully researched profile of acquittal rates it is still a matter of very difficult and subjective judgment to decide whether a given rate is "too high". Social policy should certainly not be founded upon the policeman's assumption that *every* acquittal is an affront to his professional competence.

Bail

> How would you like to live in a country where 115 people are thrown into gaol without trial every working day? You do. Every year something approaching 50,000 people are sent to prisons or remand homes to await trial or sentence, 30,000 of whom have not been convicted. More than 2,000 are found not guilty at their trial and nearly 20,000 are not given custodial sentences.[14]

These words come from a newspaper article highlighting the grave inadequacies in the machinery for granting bail. Magna Carta laid down the principle that excessive bail should not be demanded, a provision re-enacted in the Bill of Rights 1689; a similar safeguard appears in the United States Constitution. But the main problem is not so much the amount that people are required to pledge as a condition of bail but whether bail is granted at all; in 1974 31 per cent of accused persons committed for trial were refused bail. Since the period between committal and trial can be a matter of weeks or even months (see p. 53) it is of supreme importance both to those charged with criminal offences and to those who administer our scandalously overcrowded prisons that something is done to liberalise the granting of bail.

The Criminal Justice Act 1967 obliges magistrates to grant bail in all but the most serious of cases, though with several exceptions (for example, where the accused has no fixed address or where there is a likelihood that he will commit further offences). Justices can now grant bail subject to conditions (for example, that the accused surrenders his passport) and must give reasons for refusing bail on being requested to do so. There has been some increase in the willingness of magistrates to grant bail, but they are sometimes accused of acceding too readily to police opposition to bail.

The problem that confronts magistrates is that they lack information about the accused which would enable them to reach an independent judgment about his suitability for bail. A study by the Cobden Trust,[15] based on 1,001 bail applications to magistrates in six cities, shows that 671 were successful. But in 9 per cent of cases

where the accused was remanded in custody bail was not even discussed; in half the cases magistrates had no information about the
accused other than the charge sheet; in only 35 per cent of cases were
magistrates given even rudimentary information about the accused's
personal background. Many magistrates, it appeared, were all too
ready to take advantage of the "exceptions" listed in the Criminal
Justice Act 1967.

What steps can we take to see that magistrates are in a position to
assess whether applicants for bail are likely to abscond, or to commit
further crimes, or to intimidate witnesses? One answer might be to
emulate the "Manhattan Project" in the United States. Traditionally,
the bail system in the United States has relied heavily on the availability of professional "bondsmen" willing (at a price) to act as
sureties for bail; things reached a point where bail bonds were being
written at a rate of $250 million a year. In many parts of the country
people were simply unable to meet bail requirements and could not
persuade bondsmen that they were a good risk; in 1963 this applied
to 58 per cent of accused persons in San Francisco and to 83 per cent
in Sacramento.

In 1961 an experiment was started in New York for assessing the
risks of granting bail on a more objective basis. Applicants would be
awarded points for factors suggesting stability and reliability (2
points for living with their family, 3 points for having held down a
job for twelve months or more, and so on); if they scored enough
points they would get bail. The system was encouraged by legislation
and has spread across America. Under the old system, 3 per cent
failed to surrender to their bail; under the Manhattan system this has
fallen to 1·6 per cent even though more people are getting bail.

The Bail Act 1976[16] created a presumption in favour of bail *unless*
there are substantial grounds for believing that, if released, the
accused would abscond, commit another offence or obstruct the
course of justice. The court must have regard, *inter alia*, to the gravity of the offence and to the accused's character and community ties
(eg. whether he has a steady job or owns his own house). If bail is
refused magistrates must inform an unrepresented defendant of his
right to apply to a higher court; such a defendant is entitled to legal
aid for subsequent bail applications. Welcome though this is, there
are still wide variations of practice from court to court; the main
problem remains the lack of legal advice in criminal cases, which
means that many accused (other than experienced criminals) have not

the slightest idea of their right to bail. It is worrying, too, that nearly a quarter of those arrested for robbery in the London area in 1979 were on bail at the time of the alleged offence, though statistics such as these must always be interpreted with great caution.

Do we need a Bill of Rights?

The attainment of civil liberty is hampered by all manner of factors, many of which have been touched on in this book. Legislators and judges, and hence the law itself, may be out of touch with contemporary social needs; some chronically underprivileged groups suffer gross inequalities before the law; the police feel obliged to "bend" the rules in order to secure the criminal convictions that society demands of them. In a country like ours, without a Bill of Rights, civil liberty is not laid out in a code; civil liberty is involved when a policeman suspects a black man of carrying dangerous drugs or when a local authority wants to demolish a "slum" which someone else regards as "home".

Some critics argue that the time is long overdue when Britain should join most other "western" countries in enacting a Bill of Rights, entrenching certain basic standards of civil liberty. The United States Constitution is the most commonly quoted example, but Commonwealth countries like Australia have entrenched rules about human rights, so does the Irish Republic, and Canada adopted this machinery as recently as 1960.

Of course, Britain already has "constitutional laws": the misleadingly titled Bill of Rights 1689 contains sections asserting the sovereignty of Parliament and forbidding both "cruel and unusual punishments" and excessive bail; the Act of Settlement 1701 contains the famous clause about judges holding office "during good behaviour"; the Parliament Acts 1911 and 1949 redefined the relationship between the House of Lords and the House of Commons. Moreover, Britain subscribes to the United Nations' Universal Declaration of Human Rights and to the European Convention on Human Rights.

But all this falls a long way short of a Bill of Rights which would empower the courts (or some specially appointed body) to maintain minimum standards of civil liberty, if necessary against the wishes of the government of the day, though bearing in mind that making the legal controls upon government *too* stringent is not always a good thing (see chapter 5).

The traditional objection has been a rather smug belief in the efficacy of the safeguards available at present, epitomised in the ideas about the "rule of law" set out by Dicey. It is argued that rights are well safeguarded through the ordinary legal process and through representation of citizens' interests in Parliament. Bills of Rights, it is pointed out, are not always as effective as they might appear. Certainly, some high-sounding constitutional safeguards are to be found in countries ruled by arbitrary despotism; and even the United States Constitution has not always been liberally interpreted by the Supreme Court.

The principal argument in support of a British Bill of Rights is that it would be a rallying point for those who seek to maximise personal freedom. As Professor Street puts it:

> If a country enshrines its freedom in a constitutional document, its citizens respond emotionally: the American cherishes many of his liberties the more because they are in the Bill of Rights – public opinion is effectively mobilised in their defence.[17]

There is a respectable body of opinion in favour. Before he became Lord Chancellor, Lord Hailsham went on record as supporting a Bill of Rights. In November 1970 Lord Arran tried to introduce legislation containing safeguards similar to those in the Canadian Bill of Rights. More recently, Professor Frank Stacey has argued persuasively for the enactment of legislation incorporating the provisions of the European Convention on Human Rights.[18]

The debate gained fresh momentum in the 1970s – encouraged by a senior judge, Lord Scarman, in a powerful Hamlyn Lecture in 1974 entitled *English Law – the New Dimension*. Contributory factors have been Britain's membership of the EEC, the debate about devolution, events in Northern Ireland, and judgments critical of the UK government in the European Court of Justice; the climate has been conducive to debating constitutional change. In 1978 the House of Lords voted to incorporate the European Convention into UK law. The arguments are thoroughly reviewed by Michael Zander,[19] who comes down, on balance, in favour of a Bill of Rights. Given the record of our judiciary and the incalculable constitutional repercussions of such a change this writer inclines to the opposite view.

8 Justice—and Obstacles to Getting It

Laws were like cobwebs; where the small flies
were caught, and the great brake through.

FRANCIS BACON

One law for the Lion and the Ox is oppression.

WILLIAM BLAKE

The concept of justice is both complex and elusive. We have already noted the dichotomy between "procedural" and "substantive" justice. This is reflected in the wide spectrum of popular usage of the word justice, which seems to embrace several, rather different ideas like "getting a square deal", "equality before the law" and "sticking to the rules". If we look closely at substitute phrases like these we find ourselves back where we started. (How "square" is a square deal? Cannot legal rules themselves be unjust?) An emotively loaded word like "justice" (as with "equality" or "democracy") may in some contexts turn out to be cynical political rhetoric designed to fool people into accepting things that are anything but just.

Despite these difficult problems of definition it is clear that substantive and procedural justice are linked together and that the pursuit of equality and fairness in the legal system is of profound importance. It must again be emphasised, however, that substantive justice is very far from being a matter of divinely revealed "truth", nor is it measurable against any absolute standards; it is a quality which lies very much in the eye of the beholder. And one man's victory is another's defeat.

In the nature of law as a contest there will almost always be a losing party, though an honourable draw can sometimes be agreed by settling out of court; indeed, it is arguable that the only "winner" in a legal contest is the legal profession. More often than not the losing party will be phlegmatic about his defeat and will not bother to appeal. But inevitably many people emerge from their encounter with the law feeling a bitter sense of injustice.

Sometimes, of course, something *will* have gone wrong; a liar will have made a better impression on the court than someone who is telling the truth; a judge will, without necessarily intending to be unfair, have interrupted a key witness at a crucial point in his story; a solicitor will have forgotten to notify a witness of the day of the hearing. Sometimes this can be remedied through an appeal, or perhaps extra-legally by making a fuss to one's local newspaper or to one's MP or to one of the professional bodies; but often, to his chagrin, the aggrieved party will find himself a victim of one of those unlucky but inevitable human errors for which there is no remedy at all.

The sense of grievance felt by many of those who are drawn into the legal system is made more inevitable by the unhappy circumstances of their involvement: they are facing a criminal charge; they are seeking divorce or financial relief when their marriage has broken down; they have quarrelled with a neighbour about a boundary fence; they are seeking financial compensation for a road accident which has crippled them for life. People only become involved with lawyers because, as they see it, they have no choice in the matter. They have their own conception of "justice" and unless they win their case they are unlikely to feel that they have got it. Their grievance will, moreover, be greatly aggravated when they are presented with a bill, not only for their own legal costs, but also for the costs of the other side.

Even a computer, programmed to eliminate human error from the legal process, could not satisfy the man who loses what *he* considers to be an unanswerable case and then has to pay heavily for the privilege. So in any discussion about justice we must not confine ourselves to the outward trappings of fair play or to the achievement of what a detached observer would consider to be the correct result achieved by due process of law; we must examine also those features of our legal system which make people *feel*, rightly or wrongly, that the dice are loaded against them.

Middle-class justice?

Karl Marx considered law to be one of the devices by which the bourgeoisie maintains its ascendancy over the proletariat. This view is woven into Marx's celebrated and complex analysis of the economic basis of social and political relationships and of the impending class struggle which could not possibly be summarised here. Suffice it to say that English society is one in which those who make laws and those who apply them are, by and large, drawn from a privileged minority of the population; though this does not, by itself, prove Marx's assertion about law as an instrument of class domination. Law tends, by its very nature, to be a conservative force, cushioning society from the impact of rapid change and to lag behind the prevailing values and attitudes in society. This has two consequences: (*a*) law and the machinery of justice *tend* to be imbued with values peculiar to middle-class and better educated people, and (*b*) much law is out of date and tends to change only belatedly and then only in response to almost irresistible pressure for reform.

These very general statements about the characteristics of law are not in any sense iron rules which can be applied rigidly in every legal context. Sometimes they make themselves felt in crude and obvious ways, at other times they appear in a more subtle guise. They apply as much at the stage when politicians translate social policies into laws as when the courts apply and interpret those laws. Indeed, the same politicians who sometimes accuse judges of living in an unreal world may be just as guilty (and with less excuse) of the same sin, if only by omitting to take action in matters which are politically sensitive. Thus we had to wait until 1967 for even a modest reform of the anomalous criminal law relating to male homosexuals and until 1969 for a long overdue reform of the law of divorce; and in both cases the government of the day left the legislation in the hands of back-bench MPs.[1]

Several areas of law can be cited to illustrate the point that courts tend to be both old-fashioned and middle-class, particularly in their approach to legal problems affecting people from working-class backgrounds. Social historians and sociologists have sought to show how consistently hostile the courts have been in their treatment of, for example, trade unionists, employees seeking compensation for injuries at work and to local authorities straying outside the strict letter of their legal obligations to lighten the burdens of the less well off at the ratepayers' expense[2]. While the charge is not strictly provable, it is certainly possible, after viewing a succession of cases over a long period of time, to detect characteristics which, if they do not necessarily amount to outright bias, display a gross rigidity on the part of judges in the face of changing attitudes and social conditions.

One qualification must be expressed towards this kind of criticism. While one may certainly deplore the insensitivity of the courts in fields like trade union law over the years it cannot be stated as an established fact that there *must* be some direct link between the social backgrounds of the judges and the apparent class flavour of some of the decisions they reach. We may think that there is such a link, many people are sure that there is, but much research remains to be done before it can be proved or disproved. Such research has been done in the United States (though even there the kind of cause-and-effect relationship suggested above has not finally been established), but hardly any in Britain. Equally, of course, we must not accept lawyers' propaganda to the effect that judges are totally neutral. A judge's background, together with his mood and temperament is bound to have some effect on his decisions, though in precisely what way and with what degree of consistency and predictability no one can be certain.

Law and the working man
There are plenty of stories (many of them apocryphal) about how lawyers reveal themselves as completely out of tune with the lives of ordinary people. Francis Bennion recalls the case of a workman who gave evidence that an incident had occurred "during the dinner hour", whereupon the judge asked him to be more precise, "since the dinner hour may be anything from 7 to 9".[3] Mr Mervyn Griffith Jones, prosecuting counsel in the trial of Penguin Books for publishing *Lady Chatterley's Lover*, blandly asked the jury: "Is this a book that you would even wish your wife or your servants to read?"

The more positive, and serious, charge of a conspiracy by upper-class lawyers against working-class people is often concentrated upon the application of the law to the relations between employers and employees (an area which lawyers, even today, often call "master and servant law"). Some trade unionists argue that judges have displayed consistent bias against the trade union movement; the establishment of the Industrial Relations Court was seen as symptomatic of a well-established tendency to use the law as an insidious device for undermining the unions.

The charge against the judges in this area of law rests principally on a few leading cases decided during this century by the House of Lords in its capacity as final court of appeal. Here are six examples:

Taff Vale Railway Co. v *Amalgamated Society of Railway Servants* [1901] AC 426 permitted a registered trade union to be sued in its registered name. (Reversed by the Trade Disputes Act 1906.)

Amalgated Society of Railway Servants v *Osborne* [1901] AC 87 held that it was illegal for a trade union to collect and administer funds for political purposes. (Reversed by the Trade Union Act 1913.)

Bonsor v *The Musicians' Union* [1956] AC 104 held that a trade union member wrongfully expelled could sue the union in its registered name for breach of contract.

Stratford and Son v *Lindley* [1965] AC 269 held that strike action unrelated to a trade dispute about terms of employment with the strikers' own firm was not necessarily protected by the Trade Disputes Act 1906.

Rookes v *Barnard* [1964] AC 1129 held that threatening to strike in breach of one's contract of employment in order to injure a third party (in this case a man refusing to join the union in a "closed shop") was unlawful and not subject to the protection of the 1906 Act. (Reversed by the Trade Disputes Act 1965.)

Heaton's Transport Ltd v *Transport and General Workers' Union* [1973] AC 15 held that trade unions are legally responsible for the actions of their shop stewards, even where such actions constitute unfair industrial practices and are not authorised by the union.

These six cases are landmarks in trade union law. In each instance a trade union found its supposed legal rights eroded by judges; the latter thereupon found themselves branded as handmaidens of an anti-union Establishment. In several of the cases the judgment was promptly reversed by statute and the parts of the Industrial Relations Act 1971, which hovered in the background of the *Heaton* appeal were repealed in 1974; this does not prove that the courts were either wrong or "anti-union", merely perhaps that trade unions are a pressure group to be reckoned with. Indeed at least some of the odium attaching to the courts in these cases belongs by rights to the politicians, either for the policy reflected in the statutes or for the unsatisfactory drafting of the Acts.

In any event, there are simply not enough cases to enable a convincing indictment of the judges to be formulated. After the *Heaton* judgment the General Secretary of the TUC and the leader of the Transport and General Workers' Union were heard complaining bitterly that this was yet another instance of the judges sitting in their ivory towers and failing to comprehend real-life problems of industrial relations. This charge is not proven on the evidence; but, given the elitist aura surrounding legal proceedings (particularly in the higher appellate courts) and the self-consciously cultivated remoteness of the judges from the world of lesser mortals, it is also a very difficult charge to refute.

It should also be noted that the social isolation of judges and the narrow legalism of their training does little to equip them to deal even with the problems of the professional classes. It has long been the case that many commercial undertakings prefer to have their disputes dealt with by arbitrators specialised in the particular aspect of business involved. Many businessmen prefer to obtain their legal advice from specialist accountants, consulting lawyers only as a matter of last resort or if litigation cannot be avoided. Thus the "class conspiracy" accusation against the law is just one aspect of a much wider problem of lawyers failing to keep in touch with developments outside the rather cloistered world of the Temple.

The fact remains, however, that in this context most of the really telling criticism of lawyers centres upon their failure to win the confidence of working-class people and their inability to achieve an image of independence from the Establishment. Apart from the disgruntled trade unionists, already encountered, special mention should be made of the law providing compensation for workmen injured in the course of their employment. Here the judges blocked claims by creating the iniquitous "doctrine of common employment" which prevented a workman from suing employers for injuries caused by a fellow employee; this rule, which caused widespread distress and disillusionment was abolished by statute only as recently as 1948. And in administrative law (see chapter 5) the courts have sometimes been accused (in the words of one famous judge, Lord

Atkin) of "being more executive-minded than the Executive".

The judicial dilemma when faced with working-class litigants was clearly and fairly stated by another well-known judge, Lord Justice Scrutton. He wrote in 1923 that:

> the habits you are trained in, the people with whom you mix, lead to your having a certain class of ideas of such a nature, that, when you have to deal with other ideas, you do not give as sound and accurate a judgment as you would wish. This is one of the great difficulties at present with Labour. Labour says: "where are your impartial judges? They all move in the same circle as the employers, and they are all educated and nursed in the same ideas as the employers. How can a Labour man or a trade unionist get impartial justice?" It is very difficult sometimes to be sure that you have put yourself in a thoroughly impartial position between two disputants, one of your own and one not of your class. Even in matters outside trade unionist cases (to some extent in workmen's compensation cases) it is sometimes difficult to be sure, hard as you have tried, that you have put yourself in a perfectly impartial position between the two litigants.[4]

The advent of a welfare state which has brought government intervention into so many aspects of life has faced the courts with sociolegal problems of a kind quite unfamiliar to an earlier generation of judges. Indeed we have only just arrived at a judicial generation the bulk of whose professional experience has been in the post-Beveridge era. The isolation of the courts from the problems of working men and women was, from the beginnings of the welfare state, institutionalised by the growth of a separate system of tribunals to deal with matters like social security and industrial injuries benefit (see chapter 5). This method of solving problems tends further to isolate the judge in his comfortably familiar middle-class world. Most lawyers have far greater familiarity with the tax problems of very rich individuals and organisations than with the intricate rules of supplementary benefit which are, for so many people, the lifeline between subsistence and virtual starvation. The situation is gradually improving, and should improve still further with the expansion of local legal centres (see chapter 9); but meanwhile one is left with the distinct impression of a system which dispenses justice at two distinct levels.

Social class and the criminal law
The problems so far discussed are not confined to the civil law. Most of our criminal law (and much of our civil law) is, despite amendment by Parliament in more recent times, a product of a bygone age when the prevailing values were those of a white, male, christian, well-educated and upper-class elite. The advent of a pluralist society containing, for example, substantial immigrant communities, socially and politically emancipated women, agnostics and well-educated working-class people, has created the need for a drastic reappraisal of the law.

Law-makers, confronted by a mass of pressure group demands, have tried to move with the tide, though such irreconcilable conflicts of interest may encourage inertia; in any event, by its very nature, law reform tends to be a very slow business, and even when Parliament does attempt a radical reform the old law may linger on in the attitudes of judges and the methods of approach adopted by the courts. Much of our criminal law quite simply reflects the morality of another age.

A black man, or a working-class youth, or a man with long hair and eccentric dress who breaks the criminal law may find himself in a hostile and alien world peopled by policemen, court officials and magistrates or judges with whom he has nothing in common, hampered by procedural or other barriers which he is ill-equipped to overcome, and accused of offences dreamed up by a culture completely outside his experience. There may be no suggestion of crude discrimination in the sense of deliberate victimisation, still less of violence or planted evidence; the important thing is that an accused person in these circumstances *feels* that justice is impossible in such a setting. This problem lies at the very heart of civil liberty.

This kind of "culture gap" is particularly visible at the level of law enforcement; there is no shortage of stories about policemen who pick on youths because of their colour or the length of their hair. There can be no doubt that a lot of lies and half-truths are told about this kind of police discrimination; equally there can be no doubt that some stories are true. Given the prejudices of the population at large, coupled with the professional pressures on policemen to make arrests, it would be surprising if some such cases did not occur. But the crucial thing is that a substantial section of the population *believes* that an arrest is likely to mean a beating and that coloured people should have as little as possible to do with the police. As the Commons Select Committee on Race Relations and Immigration said in a report published in 1972:

> Over and over again it has been put to us that what matters is not so much what a policeman did or did not do but the impression created in the minds of immigrants. If they believe the police committed an injustice, then the harm has been done, whether the injustice was real or imagined.[5]

The beliefs of immigrants and other minority groups may be self-fulfilling, and there can be no doubt that they have an important bearing on the attitudes of people in general towards the criminal law and the agencies of its enforcement.

Viewing this matter from the other side, much has been written about "positive discrimination" by law enforcement agencies in favour of people with the "right" accents and coming from "respectable" middle-class homes; again, it would be surprising if there were not a grain of truth in such a view, if only because people from similar backgrounds are socialised into accepting the same attitudes towards law and because they communicate with one another more easily. But, again, the evidence is obscured by folklore. Occasionally a "respectable" background may even count *against* an accused person in that a judge might see a middle-class deviant as having let the side down.

We have already seen how some kinds of law-breaking, such as motoring offences, are seen as "less criminal" than others. Criminologists have long been interested in the characteristics of "white-collar crime"; research has suggested, for example, that factory inspectors responsible for initiating prosecutions against employers guilty of using dangerous machines fall over backwards to accept the most flimsy excuses for repeated and serious violations of the law, and will only prosecute after a whole succession of warnings has been ignored or when an employee is seriously injured.[6] Such evidence only reinforces the widespread impression that justice is defined differently in different social contexts.

Access to justice
Closely bound up with the attitudes of law-makers and law-givers

are problems arising out of the way in which the machinery of justice is constructed and the procedures by which legal rules come to be applied to actual cases. If unsatisfactory procedures are combined with an inefficient legal system in which people are kept waiting for months for their case to come on and with the kind of "culture gap" already discussed, then many a litigant must emerge from the legal system feeling that "justice" has little to do with what he has experienced.

Medieval English law hinged almost entirely on what nowadays would be regarded as procedural rules. The art of advocacy consisted of fitting the client's case into one of the recognised forms of action and "pleading" it correctly in court. The slightest error of the most technical kind spelt disaster; and if the clerk of the court made a small mistake in recording the outcome of the case then the decision could be quashed on a writ of error (then the only appellate remedy).

Times have of course changed, and lawyers tend nowadays to concern themselves more with the substance of the case than with its form, though it is still possible to lose a good case by neglecting an important piece of procedure (the court can allow the rules to be bent to a limited extent in the interests of justice, but there *are* limits). Although procedural law is constantly being updated, some anomalies are still to be found and others have only vanished after a long fight. It is hard to believe that it is only since 1898 that a person accused of a serious crime has been allowed to give sworn evidence on his own behalf. And we have already seen how the restrictive rule of Crown privilege, modified by the House of Lords as recently as 1968, denied many litigants the right to disclosure of documents essential to their case. Procedural law continues to be a bone of contention in administrative law where it is often complained that the remedies the law provides are hedged about with procedural difficulties; the Law Commission has recently suggested a major tidying-up operation.[7] The rigid rule against hearsay in the law of evidence (witnesses are not allowed to report statements allegedly made by third parties who are not themselves giving evidence) has undergone some modification but still gives rise to problems. In criminal law we may have in prospect a major restructuring of the trial process (see pp. 114–15 and Appendix 3), though this seems unlikely.

Procedural law is highly technical and is effectively the key to obtaining justice; yet it is a key possessed only by trained lawyers. Most laymen (the redoubtable Mr Alfie Hinds is an exception who proved the rule[8]), confronted by the maze of technical rules which characterise the legal process, are likely to be totally bemused; the poorer and less well-educated they are the more bemused they are going to be and the more help they are going to need. Yet poverty and lack of education are themselves often barriers to getting proper assistance.

Ignoring for a moment the question of whether people from poor backgrounds are likely to *see* their problems as susceptible to being solved by lawyers and whether, if they do, they are then likely to be willing and able to consult one, it must be said straight away that, as with so many things, the key word is "money". Since poorer people cannot afford lawyers' fees then the quality of justice in society must depend on the devices intended to secure equality before the law for those with little or no funds of their own. This large and important topic is discussed in the next chapter.

The middle-class aura that pervades the law is not calculated to encourage poorer people to seek the services of lawyers. Many people regard the law as something designed for people other than themselves and go through their lives forfeiting their legal rights without giving a thought to the remedy that a court or a tribunal or even a solicitor's letter might provide. Wives meekly submit to repeated acts of cruelty by their husbands; tenants pay excessive rents for substandard accommodation and are not issued with rent books as the law demands; people accept as gospel the interpretation of complex social security legislation handed down to them by junior officials of the Department of Health and Social Security; they allow themselves to be bullied by traders into paying for goods they do not really want. The widespread ignorance of legal rights permits unscrupulous people to exploit others by empty threats of imprisonment for debt or seizure of their property or eviction from their homes. Every day someone signs away his legal rights by accepting apparently generous guarantees which in fact give the consumer a lot less than his bare rights under the Sale of Goods Act (though the latter problem has been eased by recent legislation).

A recent study[9] of the unmet need for legal services in three London boroughs with large working-class populations, showed clearly that people are not getting much-needed advice and are suffering in consequence. There are numerous potential sources of legal advice apart from the obvious ones like solicitors' offices, legal advice centres and Citizens' Advice Bureaux; trade unions, local government departments, MPs, courts, police, probation officers and hospitals were all found to play their part in dispensing legal (and other) advice. Yet the authors found many cases of quite serious legal problems which were not getting proper treatment. In their sample, there were 181 cases of accidents serious enough to warrant time being taken off work, but in only 78 cases did the victim get legal advice; if compensation was paid, those who had taken advice invariably did better than those who did not. Many employers and public bodies are all too willing to fob off the naïve victim of negligence with *ex gratia* payments of a few pounds, even in cases of quite serious injury. Consistently it is the poor who come off worst and who are least informed about the nature, availability and cost of legal services, including the legal aid and advice scheme.

It is understandable that people should not wish to get involved with the law; they do not wish to make heavy weather of small problems or to create unnecessary unpleasantness. In some cases the cost even of a solicitor's letter will exceed the value of the legal right which it seeks to enforce. But many problems are far from small to the person concerned, and could easily be resolved, given the proper advice; the benefits of taking action are often multiplied when a group of people is involved, as when tenants decide to take a stand against their bullying landlord.

Part of the problem stems from the deterrent effect of costs (or suppositions about costs) and ignorance of the extent of legal aid. But further difficulty arises from the fact that many solicitors have become accustomed for too long to dealing exclusively with rich men's problems, and have sited their offices away from working-class areas. To quote a Fabian Society research report[10]:

It seems that in Bethnal Green there are only two firms of solicitors for a population of 46,000, and one of these firms does neither county court nor magistrates' court work. Poplar, with a population of 68,000 has only one firm. (The national average is one solicitor for every 2,275 of the population.) Solicitors in London are in fact concentrated to a quite remarkable extent in a few areas. Of the 1,624 or so firms, 1,140 (69 per cent) are located in 6 (5 per cent) of the 118 postal districts. There seem to be 13 postal districts with no firm of solicitors, 18 with one firm and 19 with two firms.

And the report continues:

There is as yet little evidence about the extent to which members of different social classes and backgrounds are able to or do in fact travel in search for professional and other advisory services. In the absence of any such evidence it would, we think, be dangerous to assume that the poor, the ignorant and the uneducated who are most in need of help for their legal problems, have the energy, the initiative and the means to find solicitors outside their area. . . . In our view, poverty, ignorance, fatalism and fear, in combination with the present structure of the legal profession, result in the denial of legal services to many, especially to working-class residents, in the largest conurbations of this country.

Such solicitors' offices as are readily accessible are unlikely to be open at times when most employed working-class people can attend. And they may, quite unintentionally, present a forbidding aspect to such clients; as well as the unfamiliarity of law itself, many people are afraid of making fools of themselves in front of middle-class professional people with dark suits and educated accents.

The extent to which the legal aid system and the growth of local legal centres has made an impact on problems such as these will be considered in the next chapter.

Mumbo-jumbo and lawyers' jargon
The legal system is, as we have already seen, underpinned by dauntingly complex rules of procedure which must place an unrepresented party at a considerable disadvantage. While most courts fall over backwards to see that litigants without the help of a lawyer get a chance to put their case, it is not unheard of for a defendant in a magistrates' court (where things tend to happen in rather a hurry) to be asked if he wishes to cross-examine a key prosecution witness, and to miss the point that this will be his only opportunity to do so. If, as is quite likely, he was not expecting his opportunity to come at that particular moment then such questions as he is able to think up on the spur of the moment are unlikely to make much impression on, for example, a senior police officer well accustomed to giving evidence.

In addition to the formal rules of procedure as such, legal proceedings are garnished with mumbo-jumbo and technical jargon which are intimidating to the uninitiated. Some of these matters are small in themselves, but they add up to a great deal, and add to the difficulties of those unaccustomed to the ways of courts and lawyers.

Are wigs and gowns really necessary? And the stylised courtesies which pass between counsel and judge? As R.M. Jackson says:

> It is commonly said that wigs and robes and some pageantry make the higher courts more impressive, though who is impressed and to what effect is unexplained: obviously criminals are not "impressed" unless that means they come back to court again because they liked it so much on an earlier occasion.[11]

An outsider witnessing this performance for the first time might be forgiven for supposing that he had stepped into a Gilbert and Sullivan rehearsal, though of course the object of the exercise is very often an issue of fundamental importance to one or more of the spectators viewing the proceedings helplessly from the back of the court – or from the dock. And do we need a dock? How can we pretend on the one hand that an accused person is innocent until found guilty, and on the other, label him as something different from the other people in the courtroom by placing him conspicuously in a pen between two policemen? The Americans manage very well without a dock; and recent proposals in Britain for establishing a family court combining the matrimonial jurisdictions of magistrates' and county courts with the functions of the juvenile court have included a sensible suggestion that everyone should sit at the same level.

The extreme technicality of legal language is another problem, but it is not easily solved. Some jargon is necessary and inevitable in a subject which itself is highly technical; the woolly and imprecise nature of so much day-to-day English simply is not good enough to cope with difficult issues often involving crucial personal rights. Those who call, for example, for simplification of the language of the statute book are right in principle; but there is a serious risk that trying to re-express lawyers' terminology in simple language might mislead by masking the inherent complexity of legal concepts.

To some the oddities of the lawyer's style of behaviour – the costume, the pageantry, the archaic Latin and French – may appear to be no more than a harmless indulgence. Certainly, compared to other fundamental obstacles to obtaining justice, matters of this kind are mere pinpricks. But they do symbolise the aloofness of so many lawyers from the real world and their very damaging unwillingness to allow fundamental change to take place in response to rapidly changing social demands. Lawyers may not be so remote and insensitive as some would suggest – indeed many are acutely conscious of social problems and anxious to solve them; but they have only themselves to blame for their unfortunate image.

Postscript

Since this chapter was written Professor Griffith has published his book, *The Politics of the Judiciary*, which examines judicial decisions in various areas (including industrial law and administrative law): while absolving judges of making "a conscious and deliberate attempt to pursue their own interests or those of their class", Griffith's evidence suggests that most senior judges have "a strikingly homogeneous collection of attitudes, beliefs and principles, which to them represents the public interest", and that they have an affection for the *status quo*.

There has been a spate of relevant case-law, some of it arising from strikes like those at Grunwicks and British Steel: the effects of the Thatcher government's legislation on matters like secondary picketing have yet to be seen. One area where judges (nearly all of them male) have shown great insensitivity to contemporary opinion is with regard to rape, regarded by many not just as an obnoxious form of physical assault but also as the extreme manifestation of a deeply engrained male contempt for women. In one of several recent rape cases which provoked strong criticism, the Court of Appeal drastically reduced an already lenient sentence on a brutal rapist because he was a serving soldier who, it was thought (wrongly as it turned out), was about to serve in Northern Ireland.

Another topical issue is the gulf of misunderstanding and hostility between many black people and the law. Section 4 of the Vagrancy Act 1824 deals with "suspected persons loitering with intent to commit an offence": this is the notoriously nebulous offence of "sus". Home Office research shows that black people are 14 times as likely to be arrested for violent theft and 15 times more likely to be arrested for "sus" than white people. Blacks and rape victims are two categories in our multi-faceted and changing society who have grounds for cynicism about the reality of British justice. In May 1980 the new Home Affairs Select Committee of the House of Commons called for urgent repeal of the "sus" law as being "contrary to the freedom and liberty of the individual". The Thatcher government later introduced a Criminal Attempts Bill which repeals "sus" and introduces a more satisfactory definition of attempted crimes.

9 The Cost of the Law

The law-courts of England are open to all men, like the doors of of the Ritz Hotel.

attributed to MR JUSTICE DARLING

Are lawyers really vampires?
The high cost of legal proceedings is the biggest single barrier to equality before the law. But before looking at this problem it is necessary to consider a suspicion which lurks in the minds of many laymen, that lawyers are engaged in a cynical conspiracy to rob people of their hard-earned cash by exploiting (and sometimes aggravating) their personal misfortunes.

It would be silly to shed too many crocodile tears for a legal profession, many of whose members are making a very nice living; but it must, in fairness, be pointed out that the conspiracy theory about lawyers is an oversimplification. Doctors are not accused of "making money out of people's misery" (perhaps lawyers would not be either if there were a legal equivalent of the National Health Service). Moreover, it is a bit hard to pick on lawyers for seeking to maximise their incomes, when everyone else does the same, albeit in many cases with less success. The earnings of lawyers are, on average, not very different from those of other professional men, though it is true that fashionable QCs earn vast sums and that, as in most professions, some very mediocre talent is grossly overrewarded. One may, of course, deplore a socio-economic system which permits a moderately successful junior barrister (or a doctor, or an accountant) to earn four times as much as a semi-skilled labourer and three times the wage of a primary school teacher, but that is part of a much bigger and more difficult question.

We must not go to the opposite extreme of pretending that lawyers are saintly men accepting a pittance for performing a public service. On the contrary, the legal profession has been all too quick to close ranks against threats to their restrictive practices and to scotch any rumours to the effect that some of the latter may be contrary to the public interest. But the point is that the most promising line of attack on the high cost of the law lies, not in making marginal inroads into lawyers' incomes, nor even in attacks upon restrictive practices, but rather in drastic reforms of legal procedure and, above all, in radical improvements of the present system for providing subsidised legal services.

Procedural streamlining

A distinguished British judge, Lord Devlin, has suggested[1] that two aspects of legal procedure will have to be tackled before we can begin to make any impact upon the cost of legal proceedings. The first is the "adversary" nature of our trial process whereby

> each side prepares its case in secret, giving away as little as possible to its opponent. In this way the work is trebled, each side conducting an investigation on its own and then the two meeting in confrontation.

Even more serious is the insistence on evidence being given orally, which

> not only produces a heavy bill for the attendance of witnesses but means, since the judge has to make a note of the evidence, that the pace of the trial proceeds at the speed at which he can write instead of at the speed at which he can read. . . . In my opinion we shall not make any worthwhile saving in the cost of litigation so long as we accept it as the inalienable right of every litigant to have the whole of his evidence and argument presented by word of mouth. It is not a right which is recognised by any legal system except the English and those that are based on it.

Lord Devlin acknowledges that in dispensing with oral evidence we might sacrifice accuracy to speed but argues that, "if by slightly increasing the percentage of error, we can substantially reduce the percentage of cost, it is only the idealist who will revolt". The ludicrous expense of persisting with formalised legal procedures in respect of small claims has already been noted. And in the appellate courts it is horrifying to contemplate the number of days spent by counsel in reading aloud authorities which the judges could well have read themselves beforehand.

Costs: civil proceedings

The rules about costs and legal aid differ as between civil and criminal proceedings; but in both fields serious consequences can face a party who is unable to afford proper advice and representation.

In civil proceedings the courts have made a rule that, save in very exceptional circumstances, the losing party must pay his own lawyers' bill *plus* the reasonable costs of his successful opponent. The "reasonableness" of the opponent's costs can be challenged (for a fee) by a procedure called taxation, which is generally carried out by an official of the court.

The way in which the rules about costs work in practice can best be illustrated by an imaginary example. Suppose a plaintiff P sues defendant D for injuries received when D's car knocked him down. Fortunately, P's injuries are not crippling, and the £500 damages he is claiming falls within the competence of the county court. Both sides are represented in court by solicitors (neither party is in receipt of legal aid – though D is insured) and the trial takes a full day. The judge awards P his damages and orders D to pay costs. Both sides are faced with lawyers' bills of £200, but D (or rather, his insurance company) has to find the whole sum of £400, less what he can persuade the county court registrar to tax off P's bill as being excessive. The triumphant P not only gets his damages but also his costs (less the amount taxed off).

The victory would have been a hollow one if D had been legally aided; a successful plaintiff cannot get his costs paid out of the Legal Aid Fund. Moreover, the situation can be transformed if D decides to appeal to the Court of Appeal. Let us suppose that he does so and that the appeal is successful. In the Court of Appeal counsel must be briefed; each side's bill may come to £500. The unfortunate P not only loses his damages and has to pay both sides' costs on appeal, but he must also pay both sets of costs in the court below where he was originally successful. By this time the costs at stake far exceed the subject matter of the dispute. Some litigation turns into a nightmare gamble on who is going to foot the ever-mounting bill.[2]

A number of points should be made about the "loser pays all" principle (sometimes called the Indemnity Rule) in civil proceedings:

1. Cases are rarely black and white; a losing party is seldom completely in the wrong and it seems hard that he should be saddled with the whole of his opponent's costs. Only in very restricted circumstances can the judge depart from the loser pays all rule and apportion costs in some other way.

2. It seems particularly hard that when a judgment is reversed on appeal the party successful at the trial stage has to pay the trial costs as well. This is true *a fortiori* if the trial judge has precipitated the appeal by making a downright blunder; there is no provision in such a case for costs to be paid out of public funds. Sometimes during a long and expensive trial the judge may die or be taken ill, and the parties must bear the costs of a retrial. (In long cases, parties sometimes safeguard their costs by taking out insurance on the judge's life.) There is a lot to be said for R.M. Jackson's suggestion of a state insurance scheme to cover appeals where the trial court has blundered or where the appeal is to resolve uncertainty in the law.[3] It must be remembered that appeal courts exist, not just to correct errors, but also to re-interpret the law and lay down sensible precedents in the wider public interest; this is particularly true of the House of Lords. Some critics have suggested that *all* successful appeals should be paid for out of public funds, but the case is particularly strong where points of law of general public importance are involved. The organisation Justice recently suggested a public "suitors fund" to cover all civil appeals[4] and this idea has received some support from the Law Society.

3. Although taxation of costs provides some safeguard to unsuccessful parties against unreasonable demands by their opponents, it is of no help to the party faced with a large bill from his own solicitor. Lawyers' bills (called "solicitor and own client" costs) can be taxed, but items will be disallowed only in cases of quite reckless extravagance. A solicitor can usually show that an item of expenditure which looks excessive when viewed with hindsight (such as the travelling expenses of a witness who was not in fact

called to give evidence) was incurred in the client's own interests.

There is, however, a tendency for solicitors to "overinsure" so that they cannot afterwards be accused of having overlooked anything that could conceivably have helped. Sometimes the solicitor is advised by counsel to pursue a particular course and, as a recent Justice report put it, it takes a brave solicitor "to take it upon himself to say that the expense does not warrant a step advised by counsel".

Costs: criminal proceedings

The costs of bringing public prosecutions are borne by the state, though sometimes the person convicted will be required to contribute to prosecution costs (this operates in a haphazard way as a kind of supplementary "fine"). The main problem is whether those who are acquitted should have the costs of their defence paid out of public funds.

The courts have always had the power to award costs but until recently this was seldom done. The late Lord Chief Justice Goddard positively discouraged the practice. His successor, Lord Parker, said that courts should award costs wherever they considered it appropriate; for example, in cases where the prosecution had acted unreasonably. But courts have tended to regard the granting of costs as casting some reflection upon the honour of the police and prosecuting authorities.

Many observers expressed grave dissatisfaction with the situation; for example, in one case reported in 1973 a defendant was faced with a bill for £826 after the judge had decided that the case against him was so flimsy that the issue could not safely be put before the jury. Michael Zander points out that the unwillingness to award costs resulted in two classes of acquittal: "an acquittal with costs, which was clear and convincing, and a second class acquittal without costs, which seemed, to the layman at least, to leave a stain of suspicion".[5] (It may be noted that Scottish law explicitly provides for two classes of acquittal, by allowing a verdict of "not proven".)

In June 1973 Lord Widgery, Lord Parker's successor as Lord Chief Justice, issued a direction that acquitted persons should normally have their costs reimbursed out of public funds. Defendants should be denied their costs only if they bring the prosecution on their own heads by behaving in a suspicious manner or if the acquittal is

on a technicality, there being ample evidence of guilt. This is a welcome change, but its impact depends on the willingness of courts to
change their ways; there is a tendency for both police and magistrates
to look on acquittals as failures to bring the guilty to justice, and the
escape clause in Lord Widgery's directions has provided a loophole.
One's confidence that things have changed was not increased by a
case reported in November 1973 in which a woman acquitted of
stealing a sweater valued at £4 was refused costs and was then
faced with a lawyers' bill of £808.

Legal aid and advice: civil
Legal aid in civil proceedings goes back to the old "poor persons'
procedure" which, in 1926, was taken over by the Law Society.
Under that procedure people who could show themselves to be very
poor indeed were exempted from court fees and could obtain the
services of solicitor and counsel free of charge; lawyers who partici-
pated in the scheme did so entirely voluntarily and without receiving
payment. The means limits of the procedure were set very low and
there was no sliding scale to accommodate people who could afford
only to pay part of their legal costs. Moreover, the scheme was confined to the High Court and did not extend to county court proceedings.

The turning point was the Second World War. Servicemen often
experienced serious and demoralising problems, marital breakdown
being the most common, which required legal advice. The armed
services established free legal advice services; the income limits of the
Poor Persons' Procedure were relaxed; and the Law Society, with
the help of a government subsidy, set up a Services Divorce Department and later extended a similar service to civilians.

In 1944 the Government established a committee under the chairmanship of Lord Rushcliffe to look at the system of legal aid and
advice. Its report[6] recommended a comprehensive aid and advice
service to be run by the legal profession (not by the state) and this
was duly enacted in the Legal Aid and Advice Act 1949. The Act
provided a framework, leaving the details to be worked out by the
Law Society in collaboration with the Lord Chancellor. The idea
behind the Act was that legal aid to meet the cost of proceedings in
court should be subject to a means test and that a separate system of
legal advice should be available to practically everyone. The advice

provisions were not implemented at once because of the economic situation; and the provision of legal advice and, more particularly, of legal assistance short of presenting a case in court (for example, writing solicitors' letters) has always been the least satisfactory part of the scheme.

Let us first consider legal aid (financial help in litigation). Eligibility is determined by reference to two factors:

1. whether the applicant has reasonable grounds for bringing his action or for defending an action brought against him; the test is whether a solicitor, apart from the consideration of costs, would advise going to court.
2. whether the applicant falls within prescribed income and capital limits. The latter operate on a sliding scale; at the bottom, someone with a *disposable* income of up to £1,700 p.a. and *disposable* capital of up to £1,200 gets legal aid completely free. Someone whose disposable income lies between £1,700 and £4,075 or whose disposable capital lies between £1,200 and £2,500 gets legal aid subject to paying a contribution.

The word "disposable" is important because certain deductions can be set off against income and capital. Thus a man with a dependant wife and children has a higher income limit than a single person, and on the capital side an applicant can discount, among other things, the value of his main dwelling.

The award of legal aid certificates rests with local and area committees of the Law Society set up for the purpose. The calculation of income and capital circumstances is carried out by the Supplementary Benefits Commission.

The main complaint against the civil legal aid system is that too many people are excluded. There have, however, been recent improvements in the scheme, brought about in part by way of statutory instruments made by the Lord Chancellor and in part by the Legal Aid Act 1979. The latter reduced the proportion of "excess" income that a person must contribute to the legal aid fund; and it extended the £40 "green form" advice and assistance scheme (see below) to cover legal representation in small cases in magistrates' courts, county courts, etc. So far as civil legal aid is concerned, Table 9.1 shows how eligibility could be calculated on the basis of the regulations which came into force in 1980. A married man with two children, with moderate take-home pay of £100 a week (plus child benefits) might have to contribute up to £98.25 towards his legal aid (quite apart from any liability in respect of his capital assets). Such a sum might be a significant deterrent to anyone contemplating legal proceedings. It is probably still true to say that the only people who can really afford to litigate are the *very* poor who get their legal aid entirely free and the very rich who can pay out of their own pockets. But in December 1979 the Attorney-General was able to claim that about 75 per cent of the population was eligible for some legal aid.

Table 9.1 Calculating Civil Legal Aid -- Eligibility and Contributions[7]

This explains how to calculate whether a client is eligible for civil legal aid and the approximate contribution which will be assessed. The calculation will only take a few minutes, and should the client be eligible for help under the green form scheme, the solicitor can claim payment under it for the time spent obtaining the necessary information and doing the calculations. The information is correct at 24 November 1980.

The Department of Health and Social Security has the responsibility for determining the maximum amount of a person's contribution to the Legal Aid Fund. The detailed rules are contained in the Legal Aid (Assessment of Resources) Regulations 1980. These regulations give the Department the power to use its discretion to vary certain allowances. As a general rule, where an applicant and spouse are living together, their income and capital shall be aggregated unless they have a contrary interest in the proceedings. This guide is only intended to provide a rough estimate of the amount of the contribution which an applicant for legal aid may be called upon to pay. If solicitors find that an applicant is being required to make a higher contribution than the calculation below would give, it is possible to ask for a reassessment.

Income
1. Take weekly household income net of tax and national insurance contributions, but including child benefit.
2. Deduct "reasonable expenses incurred in connection with employment" e.g. travelling expenses, trade union dues, reasonable childminding payments incurred during absence at work.
3. Deduct weekly rent or mortgage repayments.
4. If spouses living together and, if spouse maintained, deduct for maintained spouse £24.45.

5. For dependants deduct as follows:

For child under 11	£10.95
11 – 15	£16.35
16 – 17	£19.65
over 18	£25.60

NB. These are 50 per cent above supplementary benefit rates and are changed in November of each year.

6. If any income is derived from interest, dividends, industrial injuries disablement benefit for example (but not from earnings, maintenance, child benefit or family income supplement) deduct £4 of such income.
7. This sum is now net weekly disposable income. Multiply by 52 to obtain yearly disposable income.
8. If yearly disposable income is over £4,075, the client is probably not eligible for legal aid.
9. If yearly disposable income is under £1,700, the client is eligible and pays no contribution out of income.
10. If yearly disposable income is between £1,700 and £4,075 then deduct £1,700 from yearly disposable income, and take one-quarter of the balance.
11. The resulting figure is the appropriate maximum contribution out of income.

Capital
1. Take all capital resources into account whether in the form of:
   a. cash savings, bank accounts, national saving certificates, shares, etc.
   b. sums that could be borrowed on the security of insurance policies.
   c. the fair realisable value of items of value, e.g. boat, caravan, jewellery (excluding wedding and engagement rings), antiques, etc.
   d. sums which could be withdrawn from a business or borrowed on the assets of a business without impairing its profitability or commercial credit.

but disregard:
   a. household furniture, articles of personal clothing and personal tools and equipment of trade.
   b. value of owner-occupied house.
   c. subject matter of the dispute.
2. The sum now obtained is the disposable capital.
3. If disposable capital is over £2,500 legal aid may be refused.
4. If disposable capital is under £1,200, client is eligible and pays no contribution from capital.
5. If disposable capital is over £1,200, maximum contribution out of capital is whole amount above £1,200.

Example

A married man earning a *net* income (i.e. after deducting tax and national insurance contributions) of £100 per week. His rent is £11, rates are £3 and work expenses are £3.50. He has a wife who has no earnings and 2 children aged 9 & 12.

Total income: Earnings (net) £100; Child benefit £9.50 =   £109.50
less Wife £24.45; child aged 9 £10.95; child aged 12 £16.35;
     rent £11; rates £3; work expenses £3.50 =   £69.25

Thus weekly disposable income equals £40.25. Multiply this by 52 to obtain yearly disposable income of £2,093 less disregard of £1,700 gives £393.

One quarter of this figure (£393) equals maximum contribution from income of £98.25.

Another complaint about legal aid is that it is not generally available in administrative tribunals, though, as we have seen, there is a less clearcut case for encouraging formal legal representation in tribunals. The remedy here probably lies less in extending legal aid than in expanding the system of legal advice and permitting tribunals to grant parties such expenses as appear appropriate in particular cases (see Appendix 2, para. 6).

The last complaint is that only very rarely can a successful party who is not legally aided get his costs from the Legal Aid Fund when the other party is legally aided. The Legal Aid Act 1974 (s. 13) makes limited provision for non-legally aided defendants (not plaintiffs) to be paid costs, but only in very narrowly defined circumstances; during 1977–78 only £72,567 was paid to defendants under the provisions of the 1974 Act, out of a total expenditure of £43 million.

Legal advice and assistance

For every legal problem taken to court there are hundreds of others where the citizen needs advice from someone who has experience of the law or perhaps some help with the writing of a letter coherently setting out his grievance. Legal advice and assistance need not necessarily come from lawyers; we have already seen that a multitude of agencies, from Citizens' Advice Bureaux to hospitals, can give help and advice on problems that may be purely legal or merely have a legal ingredient (marital breakdown is a social problem long before it becomes a legal one, though matrimonial proceedings constitute by far the largest subject category in applications for civil legal aid).

It is in the field of advice and assistance stopping short of representation in court that our legal aid system has always been weakest, and it is only just beginning to improve. Since the advice part of the 1949 Act came into effect, free or very cheap legal advice has been available to applicants on supplementary benefit or who are revealed by a means test to be very poor.

From 1959 until the enactment of the Legal Advice and Assistance Act 1972 (see below) the Law Society supplemented this statutory provision with a voluntary scheme under which anyone, regardless of means, could select a solicitor from a panel of those willing to take part in the scheme and get half an hour of advice for a fee of £1.

We have seen that there is still a very large unmet need for legal services and this stems, at least in part, from the "cultural" and other obstacles to obtaining justice, noted in the last chapter. But there is another problem. The system provides for legal advice and it provides for legal aid in litigation; but quite a lot of problems fall between the two. A great deal can often be achieved, for example, by a judiciously phrased solicitor's letter.

The 1949 Act provided such intermediate legal assistance, but tied it to the same cumbersome rigmarole of a means test and application to legal aid committees as is necessary to get full legal aid. By the time the certificate came through the problem had either resolved itself (probably to the detriment of the applicant) or festered into a state where litigation was the only remedy. Small wonder that this part of the service was very little used.

In 1968 the Law Society proposed establishing a "£25 scheme", which would enable solicitors to do up to £25-worth of non-litigious work for a client after a simple on-the-spot means test, without first having to get a certificate. Coupled to this was a proposal for the appointment of solicitors to act as liaison officers to ensure that people visiting advisory bodies such as Citizens' Advice Bureaux could be channelled to solicitors qualified to handle their problems. In a later memorandum it also recommended setting up permanent legal advice centres (see below). An experimental liaison scheme began in Camden in 1969.

After some procrastination the proposals were implemented in the Legal Advice and Assistance Act 1972. The £25 scheme came into effect in April 1973, but the government postponed implementing the provisions relating to advice centres and to liaison officers until the full effects of the £25 scheme had been tested. Evidence suggests that the new scheme has done little to deflect solicitors into the fields of welfare rights and tribunals and that (despite extensive advertising) the take-up rate has been disappointing. On 1 October 1980 the £25 limit was raised to £40, a change which was long overdue, though the new figure by no means reflects the inflation that has occurred since the original figure was set.

Neighbourhood law centres

Another significant document published in 1968 was the Fabian Tract, *Justice for All* which exposed the yawning gaps in the provision of legal services for the less well-off. It pointed an approving finger at the American "neighbourhood law firm" in which salaried lawyers provide a comprehensive service of advice and assistance in a community setting.[8]

Such advice centres are by no means unknown in Britain. Old university settlements like Toynbee Hall in the East End of London have for many years been dispensing free advice; and much of the advice given by Citizens' Advice Bureaux and other agencies is "legal" in character. But the last few years have seen a growth of legal centres, particularly in poorer urban areas like North Kensington, with the encouragement of local solicitors and with financial support from charitable foundations, local authorities, and even from the Central Government via its urban aid programme. Such bodies, manned by volunteers, though usually with a salaried solicitor in permanent attendance, are not constrained by statutory means tests; as well as giving advice and assistance they can provide much-needed representation before tribunals. There has been a huge expansion of law centres and voluntary legal advice centres: by the late 1970s there were 27 of the former and 130 of the latter.[9]

Towards a national legal service?

In 1970 the Labour Lord Chancellor, Lord Gardiner, was asked by the editor of the *New Law Journal* what he thought of the idea of expanding the legal aid system to provide "aid wherever there is need, as in the case of health under the National Health Service".[10] He replied:

Well, I would not think so really. Health is a good thing and to be fostered, but litigation is not really good or to be encouraged. Legal aid is a service like any other service, and I am not sure really why people should expect to have legal services for nothing.

Lord Gardiner is by no means the first person to deploy this argument, but it seems to confuse *means* with *ends*. "Health" is surely more closely analogous to "absence of legal worries" than to "litigation"; litigation is much more akin to "surgical operations", and it hardly makes much sense to condemn the National Health Service for "encouraging" more operations. Nor would one abandon the Health Service because a few hypochondriacs make use of its facilities.

In the 1973–74 Estimates Parliament was asked to vote more than £2,000 million to the National Health Service and about £25 million to the Legal Aid Fund. A straightforward comparison between these two figures cannot be made (for example, the health figure includes sums spent on hospital buildings and ancillary staff; the legal aid figure relates only to lawyers' fees and not to the provision of court buildings and the salaries of judges). But even if it could, and there remained a vast disparity between the two figures, it would be a matter for complex political judgment whether the order of priorities was "right" or "wrong". And even if we argue that the state spends too little on its legal services it is another matter to make out a cast-iron case for a national legal service.

Critics like Lord Gardiner may well be right, though perhaps for the wrong reasons. A comprehensive national legal service might stretch the resources of the legal profession to breaking point – there may not be enough lawyers to go around. Moreover, as we have seen, there is a strong case for saying that legal assistance by itself is not enough. What is needed is a better integration of legal advice and assistance machinery on the one hand, and the social services on the other.

The legal profession would implacably resist having its internal affairs run by the state (as indeed would the doctors), and the political resistance to a national legal service would be formidable. There is, however, a growing awareness among lawyers of the special problems facing the more deprived sections of the community and much more professional encouragment than in the past for local legal centres. The 1972 Act is a welcome step in the right direction. There is still a long way to go, but the best prospects for improvement lie in a comprehensive system of legal centres, well publicised, cutting across the unreal boundary between "legal" and "social" problems, operating flexibly and without constant recourse to invidious and rigid means tests.

Legal aid: criminal

The idea of an accused person being represented in criminal proceedings is quite modern. Until 1836 a person charged with felony (the most serious crimes) could not be represented even if he could afford an advocate's fee; it was as recently as 1898 that an accused person was first allowed to give sworn evidence on his own behalf. The nearest thing to legal aid was the "dock brief" which entitled a prisoner who could produce a fee of one guinea to claim the services of any barrister wigged and robed in the court at that time.

The first breakthrough was the Poor Prisoners' Defence Act 1903 which gave free representation in trials on indictment. But no financial help was available in committal proceedings or in cases tried summarily. Moreover, the magistrates who considered the application had to satisfy themselves that the accused had a worthwhile defence to the charge; this meant not only that the court had to prejudge the issue but also that the accused had to disclose his defence at an early stage, thus giving the prosecution a tactical advantage.

A committee reported on the subject in 1926 and recommended extension of the 1903 Act to committals and summary trials. The Poor Prisoners' Defence Act 1930 abolished the "disclosure" rule and extended legal aid to proceedings before magistrates. But many magistrates remained resistant to the idea of "squandering public money on criminals" and often seemed unaware that they were no longer entitled to insist upon disclosure of the defence.

The parts of the Legal Aid and Advice Act 1949 dealing with criminal legal aid did not become fully operative until the early 1960s. Meanwhile, the 1930 Act, albeit amended, continued to be the basis of criminal legal aid. In 1966 a committee, chaired by Mr Justice (later Lord Chief Justice) Widgery, recommended drastic changes;[11] its proposals were substantially enacted in the Criminal Justice Act 1967.

The three main aspects considered by the Widgery Committee were:

1. Who should decide applications for legal aid? On the civil side, as we have seen, the task is entrusted to legal aid committees, but criminal legal aid has always been dealt with by the courts themselves. Some witnesses advocated taking the decision away from the courts on the grounds that it involves their making prejudgments about the merits of an applicant's case. The Committee took the view that transferring the decision to an outside body would cause inordinate trouble and delay.
2. Who should assess an applicant's financial means? This had always been done by the court itself and the Committee rejected the idea of transferring the task to the Supplementary Benefits Commission, as in civil legal aid. Hitherto, the assessment of means had been done on a very rough-and-ready basis; the Committee proposed that applicants should fill in a detailed form and, where considered necessary, pay a down-payment on their contribution (see below).
3. Should those in receipt of legal aid be required to pay a contribution if they can afford to do so? Until the 1967 Act, criminal legal aid was awarded on an all or nothing basis; the Act implemented the Widgery Committee's recommendation that contributions should be payable.

(It is interesting to note that there are no statutory income and capital limits in criminal legal aid, but in practice eligibility is based on similar criteria to those that apply on the civil side, though without an upper limit for capital.)

There is ostensibly a sort of rough justice in requiring convicted criminals to pay something towards the costs of their defence; the new rule about the payment of costs to persons who are acquitted normally exempts such people from making legal aid contributions. But opponents of the new arrangements point out that, even before the 1967 Act, about two-thirds of those refused legal aid because their means were too great did not spend their supposed "wealth" on legal representation; this suggests that the prospect of a contribution may deter people of modest means from applying for the legal help that they need. Since the actual assessment of eligibility is not made until the trial is over people do not know in advance exactly how much they are going to be asked to contribute.

There are some indications that this part of the Act is not working well. Figures collected by the Institute of Judicial Administration in Birmingham suggest that hardly any of those who apply for legal aid are found liable to contribute; they found that only about 5 per cent of the total cost of criminal legal aid is recouped from contributions.

The courts and criminal legal aid

In recent years the courts have, on the whole, become a little more willing to grant legal aid. Lord Chief Justice Goddard caused a decline during the 1950s when he suggested that courts were being too generous; but Lord Chief Justice Parker improved matters by stressing that legal aid should be awarded more generously and that the accused should always be given the opportunity to have legal representation where the court intended to impose a custodial penalty. The Criminal Justice Act 1972 provides that an unrepresented person cannot be sent to prison, or to Borstal or to a detention centre (unless he has been sentenced to the same punishment on a previous occasion) without first being told of his right to legal aid and given proper opportunity to apply for it; but the Act does not compel the court to *grant* such applications.

The impact of the 1972 Act is hard to measure. A disturbing amount of evidence has been collected in recent years of wide variations in the policies of different courts towards the granting of legal aid. The pioneering research on this subject was carried out by Michael Zander in association with the Cobden trust.[12] In a survey of criminal courts in London in 1969, Zander discovered that in only 21 per cent of cases tried summarily by magistrates (he excluded minor motoring offences) was the accused represented, and only one-fifth of these defendants had paid for that representation out of their own pockets. Representation was much more frequent in trials on indictment. There were huge variations between different courts; in Willesden magistrates' court only 13 per cent were represented, compared with 48 per cent in Highgate. Table 9.2 shows that a significant proportion of those not represented received custodial sentences, large fines, or were disqualified from driving (though in many cases legal representation as such would have been of little use because for some offences, like drunken driving, disqualification is mandatory).

Subsequent research has confirmed that this situation is not confined to London. A table printed in *Hansard* in July 1971[13] revealed some spectacular disparities. In Manchester only 7 per cent of applicants in summary proceedings were refused, compared with 56 per cent in Birmingham. Justices in the City of Oxford refused 31 per cent of applications, while the Oxfordshire County Justices refused 9 per cent. Many Benches recorded no refusals in applications relating to committal proceedings; Birkenhead refused thirty applications out of ninety.

Variations such as these are gravely disquieting though they may signify, for example, the differing propensities of magistrates' courts (and their clerks) to encourage formal applications for legal aid even in cases where the application is likely to fail. But there is much to be said for the views expressed by the National Council for Civil Liberties that legal aid should be available as of right in all cases where the accused stands to lose his liberty or his livelihood or where either the technical nature of the proceedings or some disablement suffered by the accused makes it unlikely that he will get a fair trial unless represented. It also suggests that magistrates should give reasons for their refusal of legal aid. The latter proposal was echoed in a recent report by the Law Society deploring the gross lack of uniformity of practice in magistrates' courts.

Duty solicitors

The Law Society has also proposed that there should be a system of "duty solicitors" in all courts, organised by local law societies, with the purpose of advising defendants who are unrepresented. A variation on this theme was also proposed by Justice in a report on *The Unrepresented Defendant in Magistrates' Courts*, published in 1971; this went further than the Law Society by suggesting that duty solicitors should be able to act as advocates on behalf of accused persons. Such a scheme already existed in Scotland and worked both effectively and cheaply; the cost per defendant averaged about £2.50.

Many defendants are completely bewildered by the trial situation and need someone to set them on the right road – if only to tell them whether they should apply for legal aid. The Widgery Committee rejected such a system, but the legal profession has become much more receptive to this kind of idea in recent years. In April 1973 an experimental duty solicitor scheme was started in Hendon, run in cooperation with the local Citizens' Advice Bureau; the service includes limited representation, covering applications for legal aid and pleas in mitigation of sentence when the accused pleads guilty. By April 1979 there were 107 such schemes (see Appendix 2, para. 4).

Litigants in person and "McKenzie men"

It generally pays to have a lawyer to speak up for one in court, but there is nothing to stop a party in either civil or criminal proceedings

Table 9.2 Sentences imposed in magistrates' courts and numbers and percentages of defendants represented

Sentence (*in order of frequency*)	Represented No.	%	Unrepresented No.	%	Total
Fines under £10	5	3	162	97	167
Fines between £10 and £49	36	24	114	76	150
Conditional or absolute discharge or binding over	15	20	57	80	72
Disqualifications from driving and fine	6	15	33	85	39
Fines between £50 and £99	6	23	20	77	26˙
Suspended prison sentence of over 3 but under 6 months	6	26	17	74	23
Probation	6	27	16	73	22
Suspended prison sentence of over 6 but under 12 months	5	27	13	73	18
Prison sentences of over 6 but under 12 months	7	47	8	53	15
Detention centre	0	0	6	100	6
Prison sentence of over 3 but under 6 months	1	20	4	80	5
Fines of over £100	2	50	2	50	4
Suspended prison sentence of 12 months	1	33	2	66	3
Prison sentence of 12 months or more	2	100	0	0	2
Prison sentence of up to 1 month	0	0	2	100	2
Total					554

Source. M. Zander, *Criminal Law Review*, 1969.

from presenting his own case; some intrepid people (like the late Colonel Wintle) have fought all the way to the House of Lords – and won. Although the courts usually do all they can to ease the path of the litigant in person, the dice are weighted against him.

And there is one obstacle which is of particular importance in the context of this chapter. A litigant in person who wins his case can only claim costs from the other side in respect of his out-of-pocket expenses; he gets nothing for the time he has spent preparing and arguing the case. This rule was confirmed by the Court of Appeal in *Buckland* v *Watts*[14] where a shopkeeper whose business had suffered because of the time he had spent on preparing his case, tried unsuccessfully to offset his losses at the modest rate of ten shillings an hour. It seems that litigants in person as well as fighting against difficult odds, must pay dearly for the privilege of dispensing with lawyers.

More heartening is the case of *McKenzie* v *McKenzie*[15] in which the Court of Appeal upheld the right of an unrepresented defendant in a divorce case to have a friend with him in court to prompt and assist him in presenting his case. This ruling enables (for example) social workers to accompany their clients to court and act as "McKenzie men" by assisting them without actually acting as advocates.[16] In fact both county courts and magistrates' courts are empowered to allow people who are not lawyers (for example, social workers) to speak on behalf of people appearing in court; this gives considerable scope for lay assistance to fill at least some of the yawning gaps in the official machinery of legal aid and advice.

Appendix 1: Looking up Legal Sources

Law Reports

As indicated in chapter 3 the judicial precedents that make up the English Common Law are recorded in law reports. There are numerous series of reports, of which the reader is most likely to encounter two: the semi-official *Law Reports*, published by the Incorporated Council of Law Reporting for England and Wales, and the *All England Law Reports*, published by Butterworths Ltd.

The *Law Reports* are divided up in a way which newcomers to the subject may find confusing. Each week a slim volume of *Weekly Law Reports* (WLR) is published and this is subdivided into three parts. Those cases in part one (1 WLR) are not destined to be published again, but those reported in 2 WLR and in 3 WLR are reported more fully (i.e. with the addition of a summary of the arguments adduced by counsel) at a later date in the appropriate *Law Reports* volume. The latter consist of *Probate Reports* (P), *Chancery Reports* (Ch.), *Queen's Bench Reports* (QB) and *Appeal Cases* (AC), the last-named containing reports of cases in the House of Lords and the Privy Council.

Cases are cited by the year of the report (in square brackets) followed by the volume and page number. Thus *Ellis* v *Home Office* [1953] 2 QB 135 can be found reported at page 135 of volume two of the *Queen's Bench Reports* for 1953 – and, of course, in the appropriate volume of *Weekly Law Reports*, in this case, [1953] 3 WLR 105.

The *All England Law Reports* (All ER) cover similar ground to the *Weekly Law Reports*, and cases reported in them are cited in the same way, i.e. *Ellis* v *Home Office* [1953] 2 All ER 149.

The layout of the main series of reports follows a fairly consistent pattern. Under the title of the case is a cluster of "catchwords" so that the reader can see at a glance what the case is about – e.g. that it is a revenue case involving the interpretation of a particular part of the Finance Acts. Then comes the "headnote" which summarises the main facts and points of law involved in the case and reveals what was decided by the court. This is followed, in the main *Law Reports* volumes, by a summary of counsels' arguments. Finally comes the most important part of the report, the full text of the judgment(s) of the court.

In addition to the reports mentioned above, there are numerous "specialised" series dealing, for example, with patent cases, criminal cases, tax cases, local government cases, etc. Readers who are bewildered by the array of abbreviations to be found in the citations of law reports, legal journals, etc are advised to turn to the glossary in P.G. Osborn, *A Concise Law Dictionary* (6th edn, Sweet & Maxwell, 1976) which runs to no fewer than fifty pages of abbreviations. Osborn is also very useful for explaining legal jargon and Latin tags, and it contains a handy table of regnal years (see below).

All law reports have their indexes, but the most comprehensive source of case references is the cumulative *Current Law Citator*, which is published annually by Sweet and Maxwell Ltd.

Statutes and statutory instruments
The simplest way of citing a statute is by its short title and the year in which it received the royal assent, thus the Courts Act 1971; as each Act gets onto the Statute Book it is given a chapter number (c.), so the full citation is Courts Act 1971, c. 23. Before 1962 things were a bit more complicated in that Acts were properly cited by regnal years, calculated from the date the reigning monarch ascended the throne and taking account of the fact that the parliamentary session in which an Act is passed usually cuts across two calendar years. Thus Queen Victoria's reign began in 1837 and the full legal citation of the Fatal Accidents Act 1846 is 9 & 10 Vict., c.93; but only the most pedantic of purists will complain if Acts are cited by short title and date.

Acts of Parliament are published officially by HMSO, but it is far more useful to use "unofficial" volumes annotated by editorial notes, such as Halsbury's *Statutes of England* and *Current Law Statutes Annotated* (Sweet and Maxwell).

One further point about statutes is that they are subdivided into *sections* and subsections, e.g. s.17 (3)(d); students are sometimes confused by the fact that the original Bill is divided into corresponding *clauses* and sub-clauses.

Statutory instruments (SIs) are items of delegated legislation made (for the most part by ministers) under authority conferred by Act of Parliament, the latter being known colloquially as the "parent Act". More than 2,000 SIs are issued every year; before 1946 they were called Statutory Rules and Orders. Like Acts, SIs are published by HMSO and listed in the various catalogues of official publications; they are cited as SI, followed by a number and the year of publication.

Appendix 2: The Royal Commission on Legal Services

In 1976 a Royal Commission was set up with the following terms of reference:

> to inquire into the law and practice relating to the provision of legal services in England, Wales and Northern Ireland, and to consider whether any, and if so what, changes are desirable in the public interest in the structure, organisation, training, regulation and entry to the legal profession, including the arrangements for determining its remuneration, whether from private sources or public funds, and in the rules which prevent persons who are neither barristers nor solicitors from undertaking conveyancing and other legal business on behalf of other persons.

There were fifteen commissioners, chaired by Sir Henry Benson (an accountant). The Commission's massive final report (two volumes of report and two more of ''surveys and studies'') appeared in October 1979, Cmnd 7648 and 7648–1. (A parallel Royal Commission was set up in Scotland).

The Report had a mixed reception: the barristers' and solicitors' professional bodies were well pleased while, perhaps for that very reason, many newspapers, academics and pressure groups expressed disappointment at the Commission's conservatism. This is no place for a detailed critique, but perhaps it should be pointed out in fairness to the Commission that a violent frontal assault upon the powerful and deeply entrenched interests of lawyers would probably have been a recipe for instant glory but long-term oblivion. All bodies such as this have to temper valour with discretion if they want to see their proposals implemented; whether they have got the balance right is not always possible to judge until there has been some time for discussion and for decision. Meanwhile the Report is an invaluable source of material on all kinds of matters with which this book is concerned.

The Commission's 370 recommendations (many of them endorsements of the *status quo*) are still under discussion – or not – at the time of writing. Here is a highly selective list of the more significant proposals bearing directly or indirectly upon our subject-matter (page numbers refer to this book, not to the Report):

1. A Council for Legal Services (replacing the Lord Chancellor's Legal Aid Advisory Committee) to review legal services, to advise the Lord Chancellor and to carry out any executive functions allocated to it by him.
2. An improved, publicly funded system of Citizens' Advice Bureaux, adequately serviced by solicitors, to give a more comprehensive system of "generalist" advice to the public.
3. A new network of Citizens' Law Centres, founded upon the existing apparatus of local law centres (p. 150), staffed by salaried lawyers, co-ordinated by and financed via a small, independent central body, and with special priority being given to deprived and rural areas.
4. Duty solicitor schemes (p. 155) to be set up in all magistrates' courts and in prisons; immediate access to a solicitor for all persons taken into custody (p. 113).
5. Legal aid and advice (pp. 144–50): a number of proposals including increased financial limits (with no upper limit) and regular up-rating; eventual unification of civil legal aid and the "green form" scheme (pp. 149–50); half-an-hour's free legal advice for everyone regardless of means (following a pilot scheme); criminal legal aid (pp. 152–5) should be available in all cases except ones triable only by magistrates (and in the latter categories of case there should be a presumption in favour of legal aid); all convicted persons should be advised on the prospects of an appeal.
6. Tribunals (pp. 84–7): public funds should be made available to voluntary bodies to assist them in training personnel for tribunal representation: legal aid should be available for tribunal proceedings in all appropriate cases (except where representation is forbidden by statute).

7. Costs should be paid from public funds (*a*) if a judge dies during a trial or (*b*) if the case is to determine a point of law of general public importance (p. 142).

8. The legal professions should *not* be fused into one (pp. 62–4); a minority of the Commission urged abolition of the "silk" system (pp. 58–9).

9. Solicitors should not in general have a wider right of audience in the superior courts (pp. 61 and 64).

10. Solicitors should retain their conveyancing monopoly (several Commissioners dissented from this recommendation); penalties for contravention should be increased (pp. 61–2).

11. Extension of and improvements in the methods of publicising the nature and availability of legal services; relaxation of some of the restrictions on advertising.

12. The Commission's research (see Report vol. 2) led it to conclude that, apart from young barristers and salaried solicitors in private practice, who are paid too little, the general level of earnings in the professions is about right (pp. 139–40); clients should be better-informed about the basis of legal charges.

13. There should be changes in the arrangements for legal education, though not a common system of training for both professions.

14. The Commission felt that proposals for a Ministry of Justice (pp. 11–13) lay outside its terms of reference; but it did moot the possibility of appointing a junior minister, with a seat in the Commons, to assist the Lord Chancellor.

Appendix 3: The Royal Commission on Criminal Procedure

Following the highly unfavourable reception given to the 1972 Report of the Criminal Law Revision Committee (pp. 114–6), and the appearance in 1977 of Sir Henry Fisher's disquieting report on the *Confait* case (see chapter 7, note 8), a Royal Commission was set up in February 1978 with the following terms of reference:

> To examine, having regard both to the interests of the community in bringing offenders to justice and to the rights and liberties of persons suspected or accused of crime, and taking into account also the need for the efficient and economical use of resources, whether changes are needed in England and Wales in
>
> i)   the powers and duties of the police in respect of the investigation of criminal offences and the rights and duties of suspect and accused persons, including the means by which these are secured;
>
> ii) the process of and responsibility for the prosecution of criminal offences; and
>
> iii) such other features of criminal procedure and evidence as relate to the above;
>
> and to make recommendations.

There were 16 Commissioners, headed by Professor Sir Cyril Philips. The Commission reported in January 1981 (Cmnd 8092) while this book was in the press. A useful two-part summary by Martin Kettle of the context of this inquiry and of the first year or so of the Commission's work can be found in *New Society*, 24 and 31 May 1979.

Notes and References

Chapter 1   Law and Politics

1. Bernard Crick, *Basic Forms of Government* (Macmillan, 1974), *passim*.
2. Thomas Hobbes, *Leviathan*, ch. 17.
3. Geoffrey Marshall, *Constitutional Theory* (Oxford University Press, Clarendon Law series, 1971), p. 97.
4. Judith Shklar, *Legalism* (Harvard University Press, 1964), p. 111.
5. See report of the inquiry into the V & G affair, HC 133, 1972; report of the inquiry into the Aberfan disaster, HC 553, 1967. The problem is further discussed in Gavin Drewry, "The Judge as Political Anodyne", *New Law Journal*, 30 May 1974.
6. See Gavin Drewry, "Parliament and the sub judice convention", *New Law Journal*, 28 December 1972.
7. A. V. Dicey, *Introduction to the Study of the Law of the Constitution* (1885), ch. 4.
8. See Jacqueline Kaye, "The Irish prisoners", *New Society*, 6 September 1973. The Prevention of Terrorism (Temporary Provisions) Act 1976 applies to the mainland as well as to Northern Ireland.
9. Anthony Sampson, *The New Anatomy of Britain* (Hodder & Stoughton, 1971), pp. 357-8. The Parliament elected in 1979 contained 76 barristers and 27 solicitors.
10. Harold Laski, *Studies in Law and Politics* (Allen and Unwin, 1932), p. 168.
11. R.F.V. Heuston, *Lives of the Lord Chancellors* (Oxford University Press, 1964), ch. 1.
12. *Ibid.*, p. 151.
13. B. Abel-Smith and R. Stevens, *Lawyers and the Courts* (Heinemann, 1967), p. 118.
14. Cd 9230 of 1918.

Chapter 2 Law, Justice and Morality

1. *Hayward* v *Chaloner* [1968] 1 QB 107.
2. Cmnd 247 of 1957, para. 52.
3. Lord Devlin, *The Enforcement of Morals* (Oxford University Press, 1965), ch. 1.
4. *Shaw* v *D.P.P.* [1962] AC 220.
5. Though T.C. Willett, *Criminal on the Road* (Tavistock Publications, 1964) has produced data suggesting a possible tie up between serious motoring offences and other kinds of crime; of 696 motoring offenders in his sample, 23 per cent had records of other crimes (compared with only 6·78 per cent of the population at risk). His findings have been disputed, however, because of the narrow range of motoring offences selected and the possibility of bias in his sample.
6. Written evidence of Sir Harold Emmerson to the Royal Commission on Trade Unions and Employers' Associations, Cmnd 3263 of 1968, p. 340.
7. *The Guardian*, 18 April 1972.

Chapter 3 Varieties and Sources of English Law

1. Such a "book" might indeed become feasible when more progress is made towards developing methods of storing and retrieving legal data by computer.
2. See Cedric Thornberry, "Why the law needs an international long-stop", *The Times*, 29 November 1973.
3. See The Hansard Society, *The British People: their Voice in Europe* (Saxon House, 1977), especially chapter 2. The Lords and the Commons both have special scrutiny committees to examine proposed EEC laws.
4. *Boys* v *Chaplin* [1971] AC 356.
5. A Justice report has recommended that perjury should be actionable at civil law – see *False Witness* (Stevens & Sons, 1973).
6. A revision of these categories was effected by the Criminal Law Act 1977, following the James Report on the Distribution of Criminal Business, Cmnd 6323 of 1975.
7. The law relating to powers of arrest is a minefield of complexities and anomalies, way beyond the scope of this book. There is a lucid account of some of the problems in H. Street, *Freedom, the Individual and the Law* (MacGibbon & Kee 1967; 3rd edn, Penguin, 1973) ch. 1.
8. B. Crick, *The Reform of Parliament* (2nd edn, Weidenfeld & Nicolson, 1968), p. 53.
9. *R* v *Jordan* [1967] *Criminal Law Review*, 483.

10. *Cheney* v *Conn* [1968] 1 WLR 242, 247.
11. *Table Talk* (1689), p. 99 of 1892 edn.
12. *Morris* v *C.W. Martin & Sons Ltd* [1966] 1 QB 716.
13. Leslie Scarman, *Law Reform* (Routledge, 1968), p. 50.
14. *Winchester Court Ltd* v *Miller* [1944] KB 734.
15. Sir N. Hutton, "The mechanics of law reform", *Modern Law Review*, 1961. Cf. the Renton Report on the Preparation of Legislation, Cmnd 6053 of 1975.
16. A list of the reports can be found in J.H. Farrar, *Law Reform and the Law Commission* (Sweet & Maxwell, 1974), pp. 139 ff.
17. *Seaford Court Estates Ltd* v *Asher* [1949] 2 KB 481.
18. *Magor & St. Mellons RDC* v *Newport Corporation* [1952] AC 189.
19. Until 1966 the House of Lords was strictly bound by its own previous decisions; this is no longer the case, though the House has in practice reversed hardly any such decisions (one exception being in the area of "Crown Privilege", see pp. 80-1).
20. Lord Denning, since becoming Master of the Rolls, has tried to assert greater freedom for the Court of Appeal to reconsider its own past decisions – and even those of the House of Lords!
21. [1932] AC 562.

Chapter 4 Courts and Lawyers

1. Cmnd 4153 of 1969, para. 64.
2. Esther Moir, *The Justice of the Peace* (Penguin, 1969), p. 191.
3. Persons nominated by a court to seize assets from a defaulting party and to retain them until the default is rectified.
4. Morris Finer, QC in M. Zander, ed., *What's Wrong with the Law?* (BBC Publications, 1970), pp. 47-8.
5. There is controversy about the correct interpretation of the legislation. The traditional view is that stated in the text; but a contrary opinion is that the words mean that a judge can be removed *either* for breach of good behaviour *or* by address to the monarch for any cause. This writer is content to stick to the traditional interpretation.
6. Henry Cecil, *Tipping the Scales* (Hutchinson, 1964), p. 144.
7. 17 and 24 June 1973 (articles by Hugo Young).
8. R.M. Jackson, *Machinery of Justice in England*, 6th edn (CUP, 1972), p. 212.
9. Cmd 7463 of 1948.
10. For further comment on magistrates' attitudes and on the processes of selection see *LAG Bulletin*, August 1978, pp. 179–80.
11. Cmnd 2627 of 1965.

12. Some recent work on juries in England can be found in W.R. Cornish, *The Jury* (Allen Lane, 1971).
13. *The Times*, 2 August 1980.

Chapter 5 Administrative Law

1. B. Schwartz and H.W.R. Wade, *Legal Control of Government: Administrative law in Britain and the United States* (Oxford University Press, 1972), p. 6.
2. *Ibid.*, p. 205.
3. *Attorney General* v *Fulham Corporation* [1921] 1 Ch. 440.
4. *Westminster Corporation* v *London and N.W. Railway* [1905] AC 426.
5. The surcharge procedure was altered as from 1 April 1974 by S.161 of the Local Government Act 1972.
6. [1925] AC 578.
7. [1968] AC 997.
8. [1964] AC 40.
9. *Duncan* v *Cammell, Laird and Co.* [1942] AC 74.
10. *Ellis* v *Home Office* [1953] 2 QB 135.
11. *Conway* v *Rimmer* [1968] AC 910.
12. Cmd 4060 of 1932.
13. See articles by J.A.G. Griffith, in *Modern Law Review* 1955, p. 557, and N. Chester, in *Public Administration* 1955, p. 389.
14. Cmnd 218 of 1957.
15. R.M. Jackson, *The Machinery of Justice in England*, 6th Edn. (CUP, 1972) ch. 6.
16. Reference here is to statutory inquiries; ministers have wide discretion to set up inquiries even where there is no statutory obligation to do so (many critics felt that this should have been done in the Crichel Down case). Note also the existence of more elaborate planning inquiries such as were held into the third London airport and the Greater London Development Plan.
17. [1948] AC 87.
18. Readers should be careful to avoid the common mistake of confusing administrative tribunals with delegated legislation; although both were considered by the Donoughmore Committee, there is no direct connection between them.
19. Paul Harrison, *New Society*, 22 November 1973.
20. See G.K. Fry, [1970] *Public Law*, p. 336, "The Sachsenhausen Concentration Camp Case and the Convention of Ministerial Responsibility".

21. *The Citizen and the Administration* (commonly called the Wyatt Report), 1961.
22. *Tribunals: a Social Court*, Fabian Tract 427, 1973.
23. At present the courts can only quash defective administrative decisions, compel the performance of statutory obligations or issue "declarations" of people's legal rights; they cannot order compensation outside the ordinary remedies available in contract and tort.
24. Cmnd 4059 of 1969.
25. H.C. *Hansard* (written questions), 18 January 1977, cols 164–5.
26. H.L. *Hansard*, 7 December 1977, cols 1736–7.
27. [1976] 1 All ER 697.
28. [1976] 3 All ER 665.

Chapter 6 The Law and Freedom of Expression

1. With the limited exceptions of ministerial directives to the BBC and the IBA and special regulations that have applied in wartime.
2. In January 1973 Mr Ross McWhirter tried unsuccessfully to get the courts to enforce this statutory duty, to prevent the screening of a documentary about Andy Warhol: see [1973] 1 All ER 689.
3. See Jeremy Tunstall, *The Westminster Lobby Correspondents: a sociological study of national political journalism* (Routledge, 1970).
4. See Colin Seymour-Ure, *The Political Impact of Mass Media* (Constable, 1974), ch. 3.
5. Cmd 7700 of 1949. The report of a more recent Royal Commission (Cmnd 6845 of 1977) has led to an increase in the Press Council's lay membership.
6. *R* v *Hicklin* [1868] LR 3 QBD 360.
7. Street, *Freedom, the Individual and the Law*, p. 124.
8. A.P. Herbert, *Wigs at Work* (Penguin Books, 1966), p. 56.
9. *Knuller* v *D.P.P.* [1972] 3 WLR 143.
10. An invaluable map of the jungle is provided by Geoffrey Robertson, *Obscenity* (Weidenfeld and Nicolson, 1979).
11. Justice Report, *Privacy and the Law* (Stevens, 1970).
12. Cmnd 5012 of 1972.
13. The history of the Official Secrets Acts is set out in David Williams, *Not in the Public Interest* (Hutchinson, 1965).
14. Cmnd 4089 of 1969.
15. Cmnd 5104 of 1972.
16. Cmnd 7520 of 1979.
17. Cmnd 7285 of 1978.
18. Cmnd 7873 of 1980.

Chapter 7 Prosecution and Defence

1. Geoffrey Marshall, *Police and Government* (Methuen, 1965), p. 15.
2. Cmnd 1728 of 1962.
3. HC4, 1979–80.
4. See J. Lambert, "The police can choose", *New Society*, 18 September 1969. The role of the DPP has also come in for much critical comment e.g. with reference to the immunities from prosecution given to "supergrasses" and his refusal to authorise prosecutions after the Bingham Report on Rhodesian "sanctions busting".
5. H. Street, *Freedom, the Individual and the Law* (3rd edn, Penguin, 1972) p. 22.
6. This is the form of words used for the first caution; a slightly different formula is prescribed for when the accused is charged.
7. *Op. cit.*, p. 30.
8. See Ludovic Kennedy, *10 Rillington Place* (Gollancz, 1961; Panther, 1971), ch. 6. Another instance is the *Confait* case: see report of the Fisher inquiry, HC 90, 1977–78.
9. *Criminal Law Review* 1972, p. 342. Section 62 of the Criminal Law Act 1977 gives a legal right to have a solicitor or a relative told of one's arrest; there has been scepticism about Home Office claims that the section has been generally complied with.
10. Cmnd 4991 of 1972. The Report was debated in the House of Commons on 4 February 1974.
11. *Sunday Times*, 2 July 1972.
12. S. McCabe and R. Purves, *The Jury at Work* (Blackwell, 1972).
13. Michael Zander, in *Modern Law Review*, 1974, p. 28.
14. *The Guardian*, 7 October 1971.
15. Michael King, *Bail or Custody* (Cobden Trust, 1971).
16. See R.C.A. White, "The Bail Act: Will it Make a Difference?", *Criminal Law Review*, June 1977, pp. 333ff.
17. Street, *op. cit.*, p. 293.
18. Frank Stacey, *A New Bill of Rights for Britain* (David & Charles, 1973).
19. M. Zander, *A Bill of Rights?* (2nd edn, Barry Rose 1980).

Chapter 8 Justice – and Obstacles to Getting It

1. See Peter G. Richards, *Parliament and Conscience* (Allen & Unwin, 1970).
2. *Viz.*, *Roberts v Hopwood*, cited at p. 78.
3. F.A.R. Bennion, *Tangling with the Law: reform in legal process* (Chatto and C. Knight, 1970), p. 69.

4.   Sir T.E. Scrutton, "The work of the commercial courts", *Cambridge Law Journal* (1923), p. 8.
5.   *Police – Immigrant Relations*, HC 471-1, 1972–73.
6.   See, for example, W.G. Carson, "Some sociological aspects of strict liability and the enforcement of factory legislation", *Modern Law Review*, 1970, p. 396.
7.   Law Commission, Working Paper No. 40, 1972. See p. 90, above.
8.   See p. 31, much can be learned from Mr A. Hinds's racy, but hardly detached, account of his adventures, *Contempt of Court* (new edn, Panther, 1971).
9.   B. Abel-Smith, M. Zander and R. Brooke, *Legal Problems and the Citizen* (Heinemann Educational, 1973).
10. *Justice for All*, Fabian Research Series No. 273, 1968.
11. R.M. Jackson, *The Machinery of Justice in England* (Cambridge University Press, 6th edn, 1972), p. 555.

Chapter 9 The Cost of the Law

1.   In M. Zander, ed, *What's Wrong with the Law?* (BBC Publications, 1970, pp. 75–6. See also Lord Devlin, *The Judge* (Oxford University Press, 1979).
2.   A spectacular instance of this is cited in Jackson, *"The Machinery of Justice"*, p. 425, n.1.
3.   *Ibid.*, p. 426.
4.   *A Proposal for a Suitors' Fund* (Justice report, 1969).
5.   M'chael Zander in *The Guardian*, 7 June 1973.
6.   Cmd 6641 of 1945.
7.   Legal Aid Chart kindly provided by the Legal Action Group, London.
8.   At about the same time the Conservative Political Centre published a pamphlet, *Rough Justice*, recommending, *inter alia*, that subsidies be paid to attract solicitors to deprived areas.
9.   Report of Royal Commission on Legal Services, Vol. 2, Cmnd 7648–1, part 3.
10. *New Law Journal*, 1 January 1970.
11. Cmnd 2934 of 1966.
12. *Criminal Law Review*, 1969, p. 632. Zander repeated the exercise in 1972, and concluded that nothing had improved since the 1969 study: see *New Law Journal*, 23 November 1972. See also S. Dell, *Silent in Court* (Bill for the Social Administration Research Trust, 1971); based on interviews with 565 women detained in Holloway Prison, this paints a horrifying picture of the plight of the unrepresented defendant.
13. H.C. *Hansard* (written questions), 7 July 1971, cols 407 ff. There are

more up-to-date figures in an article by Howard Levenson, *LAG Bulletin*, January 1980.

14. [1970] 1 QB 27.

15. [1971] P 73.

16. See G. Mungham and P.A. Thomas, "Lay advocacy", *New Society*, 3 January 1974, p. 16.

Bibliography

N.B. Editions of books cited here are those current in April 1980: in some cases (to minimise expensive re-setting) citations in the footnotes to chapters still refer to earlier editions, current when this book was first written.

(An asterisk indicates that the book has been published in paperback.)

Those studying the law for the first time would do well to begin by reading Glanville Williams, *Learning the Law** (10th edn, Stevens, 1978), which is a thoroughly readable guide to the techniques of legal study and the pitfalls likely to confront the beginner.

The best overall view of the legal system is R.M. Jackson, *The Machinery of Justice in England** (7th edn, Cambridge University Press, 1977), which is a perceptive and often critical account of the working of courts and tribunals, the organisation of the legal profession, etc., and an invaluable work of reference in its own right.

M. Zander, *Cases and Materials of the English Legal System** (2nd edn, Weidenfeld & Nicolson, 1976) is a useful anthology of documents, cases, etc., illustrating the working of the law, presented from a highly critical standpoint; it contains extracts from many of the reports and articles referred to in this book. See also his *Legal Services for the Community**, (Temple Smith, 1978). A more sociological view of this subject-area is provided by the Open University course-book, *Public Order** (Open University Press, 1972), which contains discussion of the concept of public order as well as reviewing the formal arrangements such as courts and the police. (The book is published in connection with the OU's course, "Decision making in Britain".)

A useful discussion of law reform is J.H. Farrar, *Law Reform and the Law Commission** (Sweet & Maxwell, 1974).

A valuable attempt to analyse the working of law and its institutions on a comparative basis can be found in W. Friedmann, *Law in a Changing Society** (2nd edn, Stevens, 1972).

Study of law from a sociological standpoint is becoming increasingly fashionable; some examples of the work being done in this field can be found in V. Aubert, ed, *Sociology of Law** (Penguin, 1969).

Returning to English law, it is important to view the subject in its historical perspective; a pioneering work in this field is B. Abel-Smith and R. Stevens, *Lawyers and the Courts** (Heinemann Educational, 1967), subtitled *A sociological study of the English Legal System, 1750-1965*. A readable history can also be found in A. Harding, *A Social History of English Law** (Penguin, 1966).

One of the traditional links between studying law and studying politics is through "the constitution"; an invaluable background source in this field is G. Marshall, *Constitutional Theory* (Oxford University Press, 1971).

A book which is packed with information on all manner of topics relating to the study of government, presented in a very readable way, is S.A. de Smith, *Constitutional and Administrative Law** (3rd edn, Penguin, 1977); this is particularly useful background reading to chapters 5 and 7 of the present work, and also contains a valuable section on "Parliament and legislation".

The working of tribunals and public inquiries is subjected to highly critical scrutiny in H.J. Elcock, *Administrative Justice** (Longmans, 1969). There is more up-to-date material in de Smith, above. A recent comparative survey of the ombudsman system is F. Stacey, *Ombudsmen Compared* (Clarendon Press, 1978); and there is an invaluable, and highly critical account of the British system, by a committee of *Justice*, called *Our Fettered Ombudsman** (Justice, 1977).

On the police, one of the best sources is still G. Marshall, *Police and Government** (Methuen, 1967), though a new edition has long been overdue. Ben Whitaker, *The Police in Society* (Eyre Methuen, 1979) is much more up-to-date, though less sharply focussed in its approach. Sir Robert Mark, former Metropolitan Police Chief Commissioner recalls his experiences and ventures many controversial opinions in his book, *In the Office of Constable** (Fontana, 1978).

The best short work on "civil liberty" is H. Street, *Freedom, the Individual and the Law** (4th edn, Penguin, 1977). A useful and inexpensive reference book is A. Coote and L. Grant, *Civil Liberty: The N.C.C.L. Guide** (3rd edn, Penguin, 1977). An important aspect of this area of law is discussed by Geoffrey Robertson in his book, *Obscenity** (Weidenfeld & Nicolson, 1979).

The debate about civil liberties overlaps with the controversy about whether we should have a new Bill of Rights: the overlap is examined in F. Stacey, *A New Bill of Rights for Britain* (David and Charles, 1973). Michael Zander, *A Bill of Rights?** (2nd edn, Barry Rose, 1980) is an admirably succinct account of this important debate. There is more technical treatment of the same subject in Joseph Jaconelli, *Enacting a Bill of Rights* (Clarendon Press, 1980).

The desirability of a Bill of Rights is also discussed by Sir Leslie (now Lord) Scarman in his Hamlyn Lecture, *English Law – The New Dimension** (Stevens, 1974). Judges may be losing some of their inhibitions about venturing into print on controversial issues: far ahead of the field in this respect is Lord Denning, whose two books, *The Discipline of Law** (Butterworths, 1979) and *The Due Process of Law** (Butterworths, 1980) are highly idiosyncratic but make compelling reading. Perhaps they should be balanced against the drier but ultimately much more persuasive anthology by Lord Devlin, *The Judge* (Oxford University Press, 1979). Lively and controversial discussion of the political role of the judges can be found in J.A.G. Griffith, *The Politics of the Judiciary** (Fontana, 1977). Heavier treatment of the same subject is Robert Stevens, *Law and Politics* (Weidenfeld & Nicolson, 1979), which is an historical analysis of the work and impact of the judicial House of Lords; see also Shimon Shetreet, *Judges on Trial* (North Holland Publishing Co., 1976) which includes a comprehensive bibliography.

David Williams, *Not in the Public Interest* (Hutchinson, 1965) is a thoroughly readable historical commentary on the Official Secrets Acts. The story is up-dated by H. Street (above) and by R. Wraith, *Open Government: The British Interpretation** (Royal Institute of Public Administration, 1977). The complex relationship between law and public morality is explored through documentary material in L.J. Blom-Cooper and G. Drewry, eds, *Law and Morality** (Duckworth, 1976).

Finally, do not forget that legal literature has its lighter side. The late Sir Alan Herbert made some very telling criticisms of the law through the fictitious exploits of Mr Haddock in his *Uncommon Cases*; an anthology of these can be found in *Wigs at Work** (Penguin, 1966). Among some very readable histories of judges and their foibles is E.S. Turner, *May it Please Your Lordship* (Michael Joseph, 1971).

In addition to the foregoing list of books, readers should take every opportunity to study the law through reported cases (see Appendix 1). Use should also be made of appropriate official reports (e.g. the Report of the Beeching Royal Commission on Assizes and Quarter Sessions, the Royal Commission on Legal Services (see Appendix 2, above) and the Report of the Franks Committee on Administrative Tribunals and Enquiries – see text); and of ''unofficial'' reports by such bodies as Justice and the Fabian Society.

The current trends in academic research and ideas on the subject can best be traced through journals like *Law Quarterly Review* and *Public Law* (both published quarterly), *Modern Law Review* (every two months) and *Criminal Law Review* (monthly). *Public Law* also incorporates an invaluable digest of recent publications, institutional changes, etc. in the field of constitutional. and administrative law. The weekly *New Law Journal* contains valuable articles and leaders on current developments. Students can often obtain legal journals and law reports at substantial discounts. *The Times* newspaper also contains up-to-date legal news and includes a daily law report. Another valuable source both of fact and of comment is the monthly *LAG Bulletin*, published by the Legal Action Group.

Index

Abel-Smith, B. and Stevens, R.,
  10–11
Access to justice, 131–5
Acquittal rate, 117–19
Act of Settlement 1701, 67, 121
Acts of Parliament *see* statute law
Administration of Justice Act 1969,
  52
Administration of Justice Act 1970,
  49, 52
Administration of Justice Act 1973,
  57, 67, 69
Administrative courts, 82, 89–90
Administrative law, 5, 6, 47, 73–90,
  128–9
Adultery, 17, 19
Archer, P., 53
Arran, Lord, 122
Arrest and interrogation, 32,
  111–13, 114–17
Assizes, 49, 50
Atkin, Lord, 44, 128–9
Atkinson, N., 21
Attorney-General, 72, 80, 104, 105,
  110

Bail, 119–20
Baldwin, S., 95
"Banding", 50
Barrington, Sir J., 67
Barristers,
  monopoly of judicial
    appointments, 50, 53, 59, 60
  Queen's Counsel, 58–9, 61, 64,
    163
  Inns of Court, 59, 63
  Bar Council, 12, 60
  "cab rank" principle, 64
  see also legal profession, solicitors
Beeching Royal Commission on
  Assizes and Quarter Sessions,
  49–52, 53, 54

Bennion, F., 29, 126
Bentham, J., 116
Betteshanger Colliery Case, 20–1
Bevan, A., 11
Bill of Rights, 26, 34, 89, 90, 91,
  103, 121–2
Bills of Exchange Act 1882, 37
Birkett Report, 106
Blunt Case, 106
Bridges, Lord Justice, 69
Broadcasting, 94–5
Buckland v Watts, 157

Cecil, H., 68
Central Criminal Court, 50
Citizens' Advice Bureaux, 134, 148,
  155, 162
Civil law *see* law
Clay Cross, 21, 78–9
Cobden Trust, 119–20, 154
Code Napoleon, 37
Common employment, doctrine of,
  128
Common law, 31, 33–4, 45
Confait Case, 113, 163
Conflict of laws, 27
Congreve v the Home Office, 90
Con-Mech Ltd., 58
Conspiracy to corrupt public morals,
  18, 99
Consumer Council, 57
Contempt of court, 96–7
Contract, 31
Conveyancing *see* solicitors
Costs,
  deterrent effect of, 57, 133
  civil proceedings in, 141–2, 163
  taxation of, 141, 142
  indemnity rule, 142
  criminal proceedings in, 143–4,
    153
Council on Tribunals, 82, 85

County courts, 41, 43, 50, 51, 56–7, 59, 136, 141, 144, 157
Court of Appeal, 15, 41, 42, 47, 58, 89, 98–9, 140, 154–5
Court of Criminal Appeal, 48
Courts Act 1971, 13, 52–4, 63
Courts, administration of, 50, 52
Courts, hierarchy of, 40, 47–8
Crichel Down Case, 82, 168
Crick, B., 1, 34
Criminal Justice Act 1967, 54, 119, 120, 152–3
Criminal Justice Act 1972, 72, 154
Criminal law *see* law
Criminal Law Act 1967, 32
Criminal Law Revision Committee, 38, 113, 114–17, 132, 164
Criminal Procedure, Royal Commission on, 115, 164
Criminal trial: adversary versus inquisitorial procedures, 109–10, 140–1
Crossman, R.H.S., 88
Crown courts, 32, 43, 50, 52, 54, 110
Crown privilege, 80–1, 132
Crown Proceedings Act 1947, 80

Davies, Lord Justice, 15–16
Defamation, 71, 96, 100–1
Delegated legislation, 4, 33, 35–6, 160
Dell, S., 171
Denning, Lord, 39–40, 68, 167
Devlin, Lord, 17, 18, 72, 109, 113, 116–17, 140
Dicey, A.V., 6–7, 81–2, 122
Diplock, Lord, 36, 106
Director of Public Prosecutions, 110
Divisional Courts, 47, 77, 85
Divorce Reform Act 1969, 19, 125
Dock, the, 136
Dock brief, 152
Donaldson, Sir J., 58, 67
Donoghue v Stevenson, 43–5
Donoughmore Committee on Ministers' Powers, 81–2
Duty solicitors, 153, 162

Education (School Milk) Act 1971, 75
Equity, 23, 24
Erskine, T., 64
European Commission of Human Rights, 25
European Communities, 25–6, 34, 76
European Convention on Human Rights, 25, 92, 121, 122
European Court of Justice, 25–6, 106, 122
Evans case, 113
Evidence, 30–1, 114–17, 132, 135, 140
Extradition 26

Fabian Society, 89, 134–5
Factories Acts, 41, 131
Family courts, 136
Film censorship, 93–4
Finer, Mr. Justice, 65
Fisher, Sir H., 68, 164
Fletcher, Sir E., 12
Foot, M., 11
France: administrative law, 6, 90
Franklin v Minister of Town and Country Planning, 84
Franks Committee on the Official Secrets Acts, 105
Franks Committee on Tribunals and Inquiries, 82–3, 84
Freedom of assembly, 102–3
Freedom of expression, 92–106
Fulton Report on the Civil Service, 104–5

Gardiner, Lord, 63, 70, 150–1
Goddard, Lord Chief Justice, 143, 154
Goodman, Lord, 62, 65
Griffith J.A.G., 65, 137
Griffith Jones, M., 126
Guinness Book of Records, 37

Hailsham, Lord, 12, 53, 58, 63, 122
Hain, P., 29, 103

Haldane Report, 11–13
Halsbury, Lord, 10, 68
Harrison, P., 86–7
Hart, H.L.A., 18
Herbert, Sir A.P., 49, 97–8
Hewart, Lord Chief Justice, 16, 69, 82
High Court, 41, 42, 48, 49, 50, 56, 85, 89–90, 144
Hinds, A., 30, 133
Hobbes, Thomas, 1–2
Home Secretary, 12, 13, 106, 107–8, 110
House of Lords, 4, 9, 10, 41, 42–5, 46, 78, 79, 81, 121, 127–8, 132, 142, 157, 167

Icelandic fisheries dispute, 25
Indictable offences see law, criminal
Industrial Relations Act 1971 see National Industrial Relations Court
Inns of Court Conservative and Unionist Association, 39, 89
International law, 24–7
Isle of Man Case, 25

Jackson, R.M., 63, 69, 83, 86, 136, 142
James Report, 32 (n.6), 53
Jargon, 136
Jenkins, R., 98
Jordan, C., 35, 102
Judges,
   appointment of, 9–11, 65
   attitudes to statutory interpretation, 35–36, 39–40
   circuit judges, 50, 53, 56, 68
   recorders, 50, 53
   High Court judges see High Court
   backgrounds, 65, 68
   salaries, 66, 68
   training, 69
   independence of, 65, 67–68
   public criticism of, 68
   pensions and retirement, 68
   Justice Report on, 69
   as conservatives, 126

Judges' Rules, 112–13, 115, 116
Judicial tribunals of inquiry, 5
Juries, 18, 32, 53, 54, 71–2
Justice,
   concept of, 15–16
   procedural and substantive, 16–17, 123
   objective and subjective, 55, 124
   administrative, 76–7, 84, 87
   two levels of, 129
   procedural obstacles to, 131–3
Justice (British section of the International Commission of Jurists) 39, 69–70, 89–90, 101, 110, 113, 122, 142, 143, 155
Justices' clerks, 70
Justices of the Peace, 11, 29, 32, 41, 43, 50, 52–6, 58, 69–71, 110, 119, 120, 135, 136, 154–5, 156, 157
Justices of the Peace Act 1949, 70
Juvenile courts, 30, 54, 136

Lady Chatterley's Lover, 98, 126
Laski, H., 9–10, 11
Law,
   as a part of politics, 1–3, 91
   defining, 14–15
   obedience to, 20–2
   categories of, 23–32
   public and private, 27
   difference between civil and criminal, 28–31
   civil, 28, 31
   criminal, 28, 32
   adjectival and substantive, 33
   clarity of, 36–7
   codification and consolidation, 37–9
   distinguishing from fact, 41
   and liberty, 91–2
   as a contest, 123–4
   as a conservative force, 125
Law Commission, 12, 13, 37, 38–9, 90, 132
Law reports, 42–3, 158–9
Law Society see solicitors

Legal advice and assistance, 148–50, 162
Legal Advice and Assistance Act 1972, 149–50, 152
Legal aid: civil, 56, 59, 86, 100, 141, 144–8, 162
Legal aid: criminal, 152–5, 162
Legal Aid Act 1964, 148
Legal Aid Act 1979, 145
Legal Aid and Advice Act 1949, 144–5, 149, 152
Legal profession,
  and politics, 8–11
  conservatism of, 11, 65, 126
  middle class orientation of, 17, 128
  division of, 58–61
  professional monopolies, 60–2, 163
  the case for "fusion", 62–4, 163
  training, 65, 163
  incomes of, 139–40, 163
  and state control, 151
  see also barristers, judges, solicitors
Legal Services, Royal Commission on, 161–3
Lewisham Case, 90
Litigants in person, 156–7
Lobby correspondents, 96
Local Government Act 1972, 78
Local Government Complaints Commissioners, 88
Longford, Lord, 99
Lord Chancellor, 4, 11–13, 23, 38, 50, 59, 67, 68, 69, 70, 162
Lord Chamberlain, 92–3

"McKenzie men", 156–7
Mackinnon, Lord Justice, 36
Macmillan, Lord, 44
McWhirter, R., 169
Magistrates see Justices of the Peace
Manhattan Bail Project, 120
Mark, Sir R., 108, 117
Marshall, G., 3, 107–8
Marx, K., 125

Master of the Rolls, 60
Médiateur, 90
Mill, J.S., 18
Ministry of Justice, 11–13, 39, 163
Montesquieu, Baron de, 3
Morality and law, 17–20, 97
Morris Committee on the Jury System, 71
Motoring offences, 19, 54–5
"Mumbo-jumbo", 86, 135–6

National Council for Civil Liberties, 86, 155
National Health Service Commissioner, 88
National Industrial Relations Court, 11, 12, 21, 49, 57–8, 67, 126–7
National legal service, 150–2
Natural justice, 75, 79–80, 82
Natural law, 16, 21, 26
Negligence, 44–5
Neighbourhood law centres, 2, 129, 149, 150
Newspapers, 95–7
Northern Ireland, 7–8, 25, 89, 106

Obscene Publications Acts, 93, 98–9
Obscenity, 97–100
Official Secrets Acts, 29, 72, 103–5
Ombudsman see Parliamentary Commissioner for Administration
Oz, 98–9

Padfield v Ministry of Agriculture, 79
Parker, Lord Chief Justice, 143, 154
Parliament,
  law and, 2, 21, 125, 130
  sub judice rule, 6
  treaty ratification, 27
  sovereignty, 6, 27, 34–6, 77
  private Members' Bills, 38
  criticism of judges, 66
  Parliamentary Commissioner and, 87–9
  Select Committee on Race Relations, 131
  legal aid and, 151

see also delegated legislation, House of Lords, statute law
Parliamentary Commissioner for Administration, 77, 87–9
Planning inquiries, 75, 83–4
Police,
  complaints by the public, 108–9
  and government, 107–8
  Royal Commission on, 108
  relations with minority groups, 130–1
Police Act 1964, 108
Poor Prisoners' Defence Acts, 152
Positivism, 16
Precedent, 17, 33, 36, 40–2, 43, 74, 158
Press Council, 96, 101
Privacy, 101–2
Privy Council, Judicial Committee of, 46–7
Prosecution process, 110–11
Public Order Act 1936, 103
Punishment and sentencing, 30, 55

Quarter Sessions, 49, 50, 51

Race Relations Acts, 102, 103
Rape cases, 137
Renton Report, 38 (n. 15)
Ridge v Baldwin, 79
Roberts v Hopwood, 78
Robson, Sir W., 10
Royal Commission on Justices of the Peace, 69–70
Rule of law, 6–7, 81, 122
Rushcliffe Committee on Legal Aid and Advice, 144

Sachsenhausen case, 88
Sale of Goods Act 1893, 37
Sampson, A., 8–9, 65
Samuels, A., 12–13
Scarman, Sir L. (Lord), 12–13, 36, 122
Schwartz, B. and Wade, H.W.R., 74, 77
Scotland, 33, 34, 40, 46, 111, 143, 155
Scrutton, Lord Justice, 129
Selden, J., 36
Separation of powers, 3–4, 6, 9, 11, 47
Shaw v D.P.P., 18, 99
Shklar, J., *Legalism*, 44–5, 41
Simonds, Viscount, 40
Small claims, 56–7
Social class and criminal law, 130–1
Society of Labour Lawyers, 39
Solicitors,
  eligibility for judicial appointments, 50, 53, 62, 65, 69
  role of, 58
  Law Society, 12, 56, 60, 144, 145, 149, 155
  rights of advocacy, 60, 63, 64, 65, 163
  conveyancing monopoly, 60–2, 163
  accessibility of offices, 134–5
  duty solicitors, 155–6
  see also barristers, legal profession
Sovereignty *see* Parliament
Soviet Union, 47
Stacey, F., 92, 122
Statute Law, 31, 34, 35, 159–60
Statute Law Society, 37
Statute of Westminster 1931, 34–5
Statutory Interpretation *see* judges
Stephen, Sir James, 17
Street, H., 92, 97, 111, 112–13, 122
Summary offences *see* law, criminal
Sunday Telegraph Case, 105
Surcharges, 75, 78–9
"Sus", 137–8
Sweden: secrecy laws, 105

Tameside Case, 79, 90
Telephone tapping, 106
Thalidomide Case, 25
Theatre censorship, 92–3
Theft Act 1968, 37, 38

Thetis case, 80–1
Thorpe, J., trial of, 72, 96
Tort, 31, 43
   see also defamation, negligence
Town and Country Planning Act
   1968, 83
Trade union law, 126, 127–9
Tribunals, Administrative, 4, 47,
   81–3, 84–7, 89, 90, 129, 148,
   150, 162
Tribunals and Inquiries Act 1958, 82

Ultra Vires, 35, 77–9
Ungoed-Thomas, Mr. Justice, 35
United States,
   Constitution, 3, 16, 46, 73–4, 92,
      116, 119, 121, 122
   law, 40
   Supreme Court, 46, 122

legal profession, 62, 63
juries, 71, 72

War crimes trials, 26
Weber, M., 16–17
Widgery, Lord Chief Justice, 143–4,
   152–3, 155
Willett, T.C., 166
Williams, B., report on obscenity
   by, 100
Williams, G., 33
Wolfenden Report on Homosexual
   Offences and Prostitution, 17, 18

Younger Committee on Privacy,
   101–2

Zander, M., 62, 113, 118, 122,
   143, 154, 156